DAVID WILLIAMSON's first full-length play, *The Coming of Stork*, premiered at the La Mama Theatre, Carlton, in 1970 and later became the film *Stork*, directed by Tim Burstall.

The Removalists and *Don's Party* followed in 1971, then *Jugglers Three* (1972), *What If You Died Tomorrow?* (1973), *The Department* (1975), *A Handful of Friends* (1976), *The Club* (1977) and *Travelling North* (1979). In 1972 *The Removalists* won the Australian Writers' Guild AWGIE Award for best stage play and the best script in any medium and the British production saw Williamson nominated most promising playwright by the London *Evening Standard*.

The 1980s saw his success continue with *Celluloid Heroes* (1980), *The Perfectionist* (1982), *Sons of Cain* (1985), *Emerald City* (1987) and *Top Silk* (1989); whilst the 1990s produced *Siren* (1990), *Money and Friends* (1991), *Brilliant Lies* (1993), *Sanctuary* (1994), *Dead White Males* (1995), *Heretic* (1996), *Third World Blues* (an adaptation of *Jugglers Three*) and *After the Ball* (both in 1997), and *Corporate Vibes* and *Face to Face* (both in 1999). *The Great Man* (2000), *Up for Grabs*, *A Conversation*, *Charitable Intent* (all in 2001), *Soulmates* (2002), *Birthrights* (2003), *Amigos, Flatfoot* (both in 2004), *Scarlett O'Hara at the Crimson Parrot* (2008), *Let the Sunshine* (2009), *Rhinestone Rex and Miss Monica* (2010) and *Don Parties On* (2011) have since followed.

Williamson is widely recognised as Australia's most successful playwright and over the last thirty years his plays have been performed throughout Australia and produced in Britain, United States, Canada and many European countries. A number of his stage works have been adapted for the screen, including *The Removalists, Don's Party, The Club, Travelling North, Emerald City, Sanctuary* and *Brilliant Lies*.

Williamson was the principal screenwriter for *Balibo* which won the 2010 Australian Film Institute Award for best adapted screenplay. He has also won the Australian Film Institute film script award for *Petersen* (1974), *Don's Party* (1976), *Gallipoli* (1981) and *Travelling North* (1987) and has won twelve Australian Writers' Guild AWGIE Awards. He lives on Queensland's Sunshine Coast with his writer wife, Kristin Williamson.

DON PARTIES ON

David Williamson

CURRENCY PLAYS

First published in 2011
by Currency Press Pty Ltd,
PO Box 2287, Strawberry Hills, NSW, 2012, Australia
enquiries@currency.com.au
www.currency.com.au
in association with
Melbourne Theatre Company

NATIONAL LIBRARY OF AUSTRALIA CIP DATA

Author:	Williamson, David, 1942–.
Title:	Don parties on / David Williamson.
ISBN:	9780868199085 (pbk.)
Dewey Number:	A822.3

Typeset by Dean Nottle for Currency Press.
Cover photograph by Earl Carter.
Cover design by Lydia Baic.

Contents

Currency Press acknowledges the Traditional Owners of the Country on which we live and work. We pay our respects to all Aboriginal and Torres Strait Islander Elders, past and present.

Don Parties On was first produced by Melbourne Theatre Company at The Arts Centre Playhouse, Melbourne, on 13 January 2011, with the following cast:

DON	Garry McDonald
KATH	Tracy Mann
BELLE	Georgia Flood
MAL	Robert Grubb
RICHARD	Darren Gilshenan
COOLEY	Frankie J Holden
HELEN	Diane Craig
JENNY	Sue Jones
ROBERTA	Nikki Shiels

Director, Robyn Nevin
Set Designer, Dale Ferguson
Costume Designer, Jennifer Irwin
Lighting Designer, Matt Scott
Sound Designer, Russell Goldsmith
Assistant Director, Ben Winspear

CHARACTERS

DON, mid 60s
KATH, his wife
BELLE, 16, their granddaughter
MAL, 60s
RICHARD, 42, Don and Kath's son, Belle's father
COOLEY, mid 60s
HELEN, his wife, younger
JENNY, mid 60s, Mal's ex wife
ROBERTA, 30, Richard's girlfriend

ACT ONE

We're in a suburban house in the outer Melbourne suburb of Lower Plenty. The house has had modifications and extensions over forty years, but it remains unmistakeably of its era, with pioneered beams and vaulted ceilings which now look quaint rather than modern. Downstage on one side is the living room with sofas. The other side is a dining area with a table. Upstage and on a higher level is a kitchen and a back entrance. There's a flat screen television set facing away from the audience downstage in the living area. It's not huge but big enough.

DON HENDERSON *comes down from the kitchen area where he has been helping his wife* KATH *by cleaning wine glasses.* KATH *is preparing food.*

DON *takes up the television remote control, switches it on and stands in front of the television.*

It's six o'clock on election night. At the sound of Kerry O'Brien on the ABC, KATH *stops preparing the food and moves down to join* DON *in watching the screen. The feeling is tense. This could be a pivotal night in Australian political history.*

KERRY OBRIEN: [*TV, voice only*] Welcome to the national tally room in Canberra for 'Australia Votes 2010', where we're ready to take you on a fascinating ride on what will be a nerve-racking night for Julia Gillard, Tony Abbott and all their supporters. A night that one way or another is going to make history. We could even see the first hung parliament for seventy years. It's been a tumultuous three years, the end of the Howard era, the spectacular rise and fall of Kevin Rudd, the worst global recession in seventy-five years and the near collapse of the world's financial system, and the rise of Australia's first female prime minister. We're well set up to tell you the various stories as they unfold, fast and accurate. We've got Antony Green's magical computer analysis, Stephen Smith and Nick Minchin—

DON: [*turning on the mute in disgust*] Nick Minchin! Hottest year on record and he still thinks global warming is a left-wing conspiracy. Not that Labor's any better. Julia promises us we'll all *talk* about it if she wins. Not *do* anything. Just have a little chat.

KATH: She's got to live with political realities.

DON: What does she stand for? What did Rudd stand for? What do any of them stand for? All they do is parrot the catch phrases that focus groups and polling tell them might win them some votes. 'Great big new tax.' 'Let's move Australia forward.' 'We'll stop the boats.' 'Working families.'

KATH: Labor's not going to rip out over a billion from the education budget like the Liberals have promised to do. [*Indicating the television*] Could we have the sound on please?

DON: Nothing's going to happen for another hour!

> KATH *takes the control forcibly and turns it on. We hear Antony Green's voice.*

ANTONY GREEN: [*TV, voice only*] You need seventy-six seats for one side of politics to be confident of governing in their own right. Both sides could end up with seventy-three or seventy-four seats with the balance in the middle there, then there'd be negotiations.

DON: Pray to God that doesn't happen. We could spend the next three years ruled by the whims of the mad Bob Katter.

KATH: Don't, please. [*She sighs. Polishing the table top*] I still can't work out why you decided to have this election night party. We stopped doing it twenty years ago.

DON: I was really hit when Mack died. I just wanted to see the old tribe together again. What's left of them. How much time have any of us got left? Remember that first party we had in 1969?

KATH: How could I ever forget. Cooley dumped the poor girl he brought and seduced Kerry the dentist's wife.

DON: [*laughing*] And got punched in the teeth by the dentist. What was his name?

KATH: Evan. Whatever happened to those two?

DON: I heard they got divorced.

KATH: Not surprising. Mal tried to grope every woman here while his wife Jenny had to watch. Then late at night you suggested a little wife swapping.

DON: It was a joke, but Mal was so drunk he took it seriously.

KATH: Then Jenny screamed at me for only feeding them chips and Twisties. [*Still indignant*] What about the pizzas?

DON: You'd just told her she was an extravagant spendthrift.

KATH: Thank God their marriage broke up. You continued to inflict Mal on me but at least we didn't have to see her anymore.

DON: Most of the parties in the old days were disasters, but for all that, they had passion. We still really cared who won. We still thought a change of government could change the nation. And we laughed and drank wine, not bloody mineral water. I yearn for a bit of that.

KATH: And you think this party is going to resurrect it? You guys will spend the night giving an organ recital. Which ones are about to collapse.

DON: Okay. Maybe it's more a case of misery seeks company these days, but there's a bonding that happens in those formative years that stays with you for life. You can say what you like about Mal, but if you sift through the bullshit, he's a genuinely original thinker.

KATH: You're obviously a better sifter than I am.

DON: Your enthusiasm for this party is overwhelming.

KATH: Just two rules, right? No Creedence Clearwater Revival and don't talk football.

DON: Hey!

KATH: Why can't you accept that Collingwood is never going to win a Grand Final and get on with life?

DON: What life? I'm a retiree.

KATH: More important things should be on your agenda. You probably haven't noticed, but your son has just left his wife to run off with a younger woman.

DON: Ten years younger.

KATH: Twelve.

DON: Ten.

KATH: [*ominously*] Like father, like son.

DON: That was over thirty years ago. How long does this have to go on?

KATH: As long as I want it to.

DON: For Christ's sake. I was back after a week.

KATH: Our son has obviously inherited your irresponsibility.

DON: Kath, that's—

KATH: [*pointing offstage*] His daughter—our granddaughter is in there. What do you think it's doing to her? And our grandson?

DON: You can't really judge what a marriage is like from the outside.

KATH: That's just code for 'if sex is boring with your wife, move on'.

> *She brings a selection of cheeses and puts them on the table next to the dips and wafers that are already there.*

Will you try and be a good host tonight?

DON: The food's there. The tap's over there. What else do they need?

KATH: You've been a lazy bastard for forty years. Why should I expect you to change tonight?

> *A smartly-dressed teenager,* BELLE, *sweeps into the room.*

BELLE: I rang home and then Mum's mobile and they both went to message.

KATH: She might just want a bit of peace.

BELLE: She was crying again last night.

KATH: I just hope your father comes to his senses while she'll still have him back.

BELLE: I don't want him back. [*Worried*] I think I should go home.

KATH: Your mother wanted a few days to herself to think. Go and watch one of those videos you brought.

BELLE: Is the player Blu-ray?

DON: I'm sure our DVD player will play Blu-ray. It'll just be a tad fuzzier.

BELLE: No it won't. You have to have a Blu-ray player.

DON: I'm not going to race and buy one.

KATH: Have you got a DVD you could watch?

BELLE: [*with a sigh*] I guess. But Blu-ray's much sharper.

KATH: Another vampire movie?

BELLE: Granny, you don't take vampire movies literally. They're allegorical.

KATH: Sorry.

BELLE: The vampire represents the bad boy from the wrong side of the tracks that girls always fantasise about.

DON: Including you apparently.

BELLE: You can be aware of the way a genre works and still enjoy the genre.

> BELLE *retreats to watch her movie.* KATH *and* DON *look at each other trying to stop laughing at their serious but precociously endearing granddaughter. The doorbell rings.* MAL *enters. He's in his sixties and is looking every year of it.*

MAL: Hi, Kath.

KATH: [*without enthusiasm*] Hi, Mal.

MAL: It's great of you to revive the old tradition. I've really missed those election night parties. Haven't you?

KATH: No.

MAL: Kath, don't be like that. Rituals give life meaning.

> BELLE *emerges to see who's arrived.*

[*Looking at* BELLE] And who is this?

DON: Our grand-daughter Belle.

MAL: At times like this one can only marvel at the wisdom of the original inhabitants of this land.

KATH: What?

MAL: The young women betrothed to the wise elders.

BELLE: Yuk.

KATH: Mal!

MAL: Sorry, sorry. Sometimes my unconscious throws out thoughts faster than I can censor them.

KATH: Still?

MAL: [*to* BELLE] You're Richard's daughter. How's Dad?

BELLE: Who cares?

KATH: Belle!

BELLE: Well, who does care? I don't.

DON: He's done something you don't approve of but he's still your dad.

BELLE: Well, I wish he wasn't.

MAL *is always in the market for bad news about his friends.*

MAL: Some trouble with Richard?

DON: [*reluctantly*] He'll come to his senses.

BELLE: He won't come to his senses. He told Mum he loves Roberta.

MAL: He's gone off with a younger woman?

DON: Not that much younger.

BELLE: Twelve years younger.

KATH: [*correcting* DON] See, twelve. [*As she departs back towards the kitchen*] Belle, will you go and watch your vampire video?

But MAL *likes her being around.*

MAL: So which party will you be supporting tonight, Belle?

BELLE: I'm not old enough to vote.

MAL: No, you're not. But if you were?

BELLE: The Greens. Everyone who cares about the future of the planet should be voting Green.

MAL: Young lady, you are wise beyond your years. We're facing absolute catastrophe, not that you'll hear a whisper of that from Gillard or Abbott. They're too scared that some Neanderthal in the western suburbs of Sydney will whine about higher electricity bills.

KATH: [*from the kitchen*] High electricity bills make life very difficult for the poor.

MAL: I'm poor. They make life difficult for me. But for the future of the planet I'm prepared to make the sacrifice.

BELLE: [*to* MAL] Do you eat meat?

MAL: A little.

BELLE: Well, you're not really green. To grow a kilo of meat puts a huge amount of carbon into the atmosphere.

Having put MAL *in his place she flounces off to watch her video.*

MAL: Getting old is a bastard of a thing, isn't it? You lust after them more than ever, but A, they certainly don't lust after you, and B, even if they did you'd need to be on a drip-feed of viagra to do anything about it.

DON: Just keep yourself a little fitter and you wouldn't need the viagra.

MAL: What are you trying to tell me? You can still stride out of the bathroom with a wet towel hung on it?

DON: Just a face washer these days, but at least it still works.

MAL: Even the check-out chicks are depressing. Their mouths say, 'Have you had a nice day', but their eyes are saying, 'Go away and die, you old git'. [*He stares at the flickering screen.*] I hope the Liberals win tonight.

DON: [*amazed*] The Liberals? Abbott? You said yourself they're going to do absolutely nothing about climate change.

> KATH *who is in the kitchen overhears and can't believe it. She comes down towards them.*

MAL: Precisely.

DON: Have you suddenly become a climate change sceptic?

MAL: No. The science is becoming more conclusive every day. CO_2 is bad enough but the big one is methane. With just a little more heating we're going to get huge amounts released from the Siberian and Canadian tundra and then we're well and truly fucked.

DON: Then what are you talking about?

MAL: Humanity is a plague species. Smart brains, reptilian emotions. Grab what you want now and to hell with the future.

KATH: You want a disaster?

MAL: Bring it on. The sooner it happens the more of us will survive.

KATH: You want people to die?

MAL: There'll be a billion or so left which is about all there should be.

DON: Mate, it's surely a lot better that we all cut consumption than six billion die?

MAL: Cut consumption? That's like trying to hold back the tide with a shark net.

KATH: Attitudes can change.

MAL: Sales of gas-guzzling SUVs are skyrocketing. We're a plague species.

KATH: [*crossly*] Some of us more virulent than others.

> *She goes offstage.* MAL *looks at* DON *indicating the departing* KATH.

MAL: Still bipolar?

DON: She was never bipolar. She just gets depressed every time you appear.

MAL: [*pouring himself a large glass of red*] Mate, if I'm not wanted here I'll go.

> DON *watches as* MAL *finishes pouring and realises there's not much chance of that.* MAL *tastes the red, looks at the bottle and nods his head.*

DON: Penfolds three eight nine.

MAL: Yeah, I can read.

DON: It's not a cheap wine, mate. You don't like it?

MAL: Two thousand and five. Fruit ripened too early.

DON: Would you prefer water?

MAL: Mate, don't get touchy. It's just not its best year.

DON: [*sarcastically*] Then let's open your bottle. Oh, I forgot. You didn't bring any.

MAL: On my budget I can't buy top reds anymore and I refuse to buy shit. [*Indicating the television screen*] Turn the sound on.

DON: [*shaking his head*] I want to put off listening to Nick Minchin for as long as possible.

> *Nonetheless they both watch the silent image.*

MAL: That's sad about Richard, mate. I thought blokes these days would have more sense than doing that old clichéd thing of running off with bimbos.

DON: She's not a bimbo. She's an artist.

MAL: You've met her?

DON: No. It's just happened.

MAL: So how's Kath feel? Devastated I expect.

DON: Until this happened she couldn't stand Richard's wife Tracy. Now they're the best of buddies. United against our son.

MAL: Young Belle is obviously very upset. I guess her younger brother has been hit even harder.

DON: Could you try and contain your glee?

MAL: Mate, don't misjudge me. I'm sad for you. Really sad for you.

DON: Yeah.

MAL: Geez, you get touchier and touchier as the years go on. [*He sighs and looks around.*] I remember that first party here in 1969 as if it was yesterday. [*Pointing*] That's the exact spot where Cooley got whacked by the dentist.

DON: [*shaking his head and pointing*] It was in the bedroom down there.

MAL: That's right. Coitus interruptus. [*With a sigh*] The sixties were magic in their way, weren't they? Hand-to-hand combat on the battlefield of social change.

> *He breaks into song, singing in tune and with surprising fervour.*

> 'Those were the days my friend,
> We thought they'd never end,
> We'd sing and dance
> Forever and a day…'

DON: Our kids resent it, you know. It's not their fault that they were born into an era of grey managerialism, but they missed the party and they resent it.

MAL: [*nodding*] Their only defence is to deride it and us.

DON: Sad.

MAL: Depict it as just 'sex, drugs and rock-and-roll'.

DON: Which it was. But it was so much more.

MAL: [*nodding wisely*] So much more.

> KATH *appears.*

KATH: [*to DON*] Do you like this blouse better?

DON: You changed?

KATH: Yes, I changed. Do you like this one?

DON: I do, really I do. It goes with your hair.

MAL: It's really great. The years have treated you well, Kath.

> KATH *is less impressed than* MAL *hoped.*

We were just talking about the sixties. Those powerful dreams, those shimmering ideals. And feeling sad about the shallowness of the generations that followed us.

KATH: [*moving off*] Don, could you polish those glasses? They're filthy.

She moves away to take out her mobile and call someone.

DON: [*to* MAL] Generation X was bad enough but generation Y's idea of protest is rap music.

MAL: [*nodding*] Their idols are sexist ghetto gangsters. It's worse than sad, it's tragic.

> KATH *reappears.* DON *hastily picks up a napkin and starts polishing the drinking glasses.*

KATH: Tracy's phone is going to message.

DON: She probably wants a bit of peace.

MAL: Tracy? Belle's mother?

DON: Try her mobile.

KATH: I did. It's going to message too. I'm getting worried. She's really on edge.

MAL: I'm sorry to hear about Richard and his new young lady. How old is Richard now?

KATH: Forty-two.

MAL: Yeah, that's when it tends to happen. [*His mobile phone rings. He looks at the number that comes up on his screen. To* DON *and* KATH] Jenny. [*To the phone*] Hi, Jens. Yeah, I rang Pete and I'm going over there on the weekend. See you there. Where are you tonight? At home? On election night? I thought you'd be amongst the party faithful? Oh, of course not. Yeah, of course. Why don't you come over here? At Don's. Don and Kath. Don and Kath. Yes, that Don and Kath. No, they won't mind. They'd like to see you again.

> DON *and* KATH *look at each other in alarm.* MAL *misses the look and charges on.*

After all these years surely we can all let bygones be bygones. [*To* KATH] That's okay, isn't it? If Jenny comes over?

> KATH *nods reluctantly.*

[*Taking the address he has jotted down out of his top pocket*] Eighty-seven Mountain Vista Drive, Lower Plenty. Only about fifteen minutes from you. And there's some great food. Yes, they've moved on from chips and Twisties. [*He hangs up and smiles at them.*] We get along much better these days. Nothing like thirty years of divorce to improve things. You don't mind, do you?

KATH: She *wants* to come? Here?

MAL: She was a bit dubious, but then said that it's about time she buried the hatchet.

KATH: In whose head?

MAL: I can call her back if you really don't want her here.

KATH: We did part on rather bad terms if you remember.

MAL: Forty years ago, for God's sake, forty years. At this stage of life you try and tie up loose ends. I can call back.

KATH: And say what? We don't want her.

MAL: She's changed. You'll see.

DON: She's become a little more… tactful?

MAL: No, she still calls a spade a primitive digging instrument, but she's only bad-tempered about half the time these days.

DON: Is she still shitty about the book I wrote?

MAL: I'm still shitty about the book you wrote, but I'm here, aren't I?

DON: How many times have I told you it was a work of fiction.

MAL: About three thousand and it's still a lie.

DON: It drew a little bit on life.

MAL: A little bit? Mate, you stick a knife in as deep as you did and the wound stays forever.

DON: I exaggerated things. Do you really think I saw you as a vain and boastful bullshit artist and social climber?

MAL: I did after I read the book. The thing that really hurt was the stuff about the size of my dick.

DON: Mate, that was just a reflection of a widespread male anxiety.

MAL: Okay, my dick's not huge but neither was Casanova's.

DON: Exactly, so what's the big deal?

MAL: The big deal is that I had believed you were my closest friend and all the time you're sneering at me behind my back. The only good thing is that nobody bought the book.

DON: We've established that point at least three thousand times too over the years. Can we move on?

KATH: She's still making fun of the chips and Twisties. I can't believe it.

   KATH *goes off grumpily towards the bathroom.*

MAL: Maybe inviting my ex wasn't such a good idea.

DON: We will shortly see.

MAL: I'm really looking forward to seeing Helen again.

   There's a wistful tone in his voice that DON *picks up on.*

   I carried a torch for her for years.

DON: You carried a torch for her?

MAL: The truth is I have fallen in love with every woman I've ever made love to, but I've never fallen harder than for her.

DON: You only did it with her once! And under fairly dubious circumstances.

MAL: That was enough, mate. It's stayed with me for life.

DON: You only did it once!

MAL: It wasn't just that she looked like Marilyn bloody Monroe, she was sensitive and vulnerable and gentle… Oh shit, I'm falling for her all over again. Don't you feel something special for her?

DON: Can we drop this?

MAL: That's where you got me wrong in your book. The truth is I'm a romantic. A total card-carrying romantic. My heart just ached for that woman. And Jenny knew it.

DON: Did you tell her?

MAL: Women can do a brain scan on you without the need for an MRI. The thing that still puzzles me is that Helen has stayed married to an insensitive arsehole like Cooley!

DON: She was never going to leave him for you.

MAL: Why not? I did once amount to something, if you remember. [*Beat.*] I shouldn't have talked about her, mate. I'm in love all over again. When she gets here just tie me to the mast like Ulysses.

DON: If she's singing a siren song it won't be in your direction.

MAL: Sadly you're right. I tell people I'm happy living by myself, but the truth is it's bloody lonely.

DON: Have you tried to find someone?

MAL: There's no way I'd want any woman desperate enough to want to shack up with me. [*Beat.*] I'm probably being too tough on myself.

DON: No, mate, you're spot-on.

MAL: I had everything going for me and now I make a pittance selling books part-time. I fucked up. And don't try and tell me it's not true.

DON: I'm not about to.

The doorbell goes.

Might be Jenny.

MAL: Or Cooley and Helen.

DON *opens the door, but it's neither. It's his son* RICHARD, *looking distraught.*

DON: Richard? What are you doing here?

RICHARD: Can we go into the study?

DON: Belle's in there watching a video.

RICHARD *looks at* MAL. *He wants him gone.* MAL *picks up the vibe.*

MAL: I'll go and check out the video she's watching.

He waves and disappears. KATH *reappears from the bathroom where she's been taking as long as possible to fix her make-up.*

KATH: Richard?

RICHARD: Tracy just took sleeping pills.

KATH: Oh migod, Richard!

RICHARD: She's going to be okay. I raced around there and made her vomit them up. I thought Belle should hear it from me.

KATH: Where is she now?

RICHARD: In hospital. She's fine. She's asleep now and they're monitoring her.

KATH: So what do you intend to do?

RICHARD: What in the hell can I do?

KATH: You can go back and live with your wife!

RICHARD: I don't love her anymore.

KATH: Richard, don't be such an idiot. Show me a man who claims he's still passionately in love with his wife after ten years of marriage and I'll show you a liar.

DON: That's a bit rough.

KATH: Let's be honest. It's been a long time since your father and I sat staring into each other's eyes, but we stayed together because of you and your sister.

DON: There was a bit more to it than that.

KATH: The passion stuff is over in an eye blink. Then if you're mature, you settle down for the long haul.

DON: You're making us sound as if…

KATH: You don't writhe around on beds gasping all your life.

DON: Hey, we still… maybe not gasping… but…

KATH: Don, say something.

DON: It does sound a bit impulsive, son.

KATH: Impulsive? Why don't you slap him on the wrist with a feather? It's totally crazy and irresponsible.

DON: Son, if Tracy took sleeping pills that's bloody serious.

RICHARD: She called me as soon as she'd taken them. She just wanted to scare the shit out of me.

KATH: That is just about the most callous thing I've ever heard.

DON: Whether it was a serious attempt or not she's very distressed. Don't try and minimise it, son.

RICHARD: Things weren't as brilliant in our marriage as you think.

KATH: Don't try and put the blame on Tracy.

RICHARD: You certainly weren't her greatest fan. Until recently.

KATH: Of course she's got faults. Haven't we all. But you should have enough brains to realise you've been seduced by a clever and malignant woman.

RICHARD: I was not seduced. I seduced her. I couldn't help myself.

KATH: [*indicating the television room*] Young Belle is shattered. And Tracy says little Michael is distraught. Have you told him about this yet?

RICHARD: Belle will cope with it better than he will.

KATH: Have you told her parents?

RICHARD: The psychiatrist said to keep everyone away from her for a little while. She's exhausted and fragile and she's sleeping.

KATH: They've got to know.

RICHARD: Just not for a couple of hours. Michael's still with them and you know what a panic merchant Vera is.

KATH: But—

RICHARD: The psychiatrist said she'd probably wake up in a couple of hours. I'll let them know then.

KATH: What a bloody mess. Didn't you anticipate something like this might happen?

RICHARD: Do you think I wanted this?

KATH: You've got no control over your bloody sexual urges? You can't help yourself?

RICHARD: I just fell in love in a way that's never even remotely happened to me before in my life.

KATH: And Tracy and Belle and Michael will suffer till the end of their lives.

RICHARD: Just because you two stayed together because you didn't have the guts to call it quits, don't think we all have to do the same.

DON *and* KATH *protest.*

You were always fighting. It drove me crazy.

DON: We had our bumpy patches.

KATH: Disputes are a normal part of any marriage.

RICHARD: Mum, your disputes sounded like a prelude to murder.

DON: That's wrong, son. Your mother and I have always had great affection and respect for each other.

RICHARD: Respect? Do you think that's what I want to be saying to myself on my deathbed? I had fifty years of respect?

KATH: In a year or two you'll find this new little predator no better than Tracy and you will have ruined three lives.

RICHARD: Predator? How can you make judgements like that. You won't even meet her.

KATH: No, and I never will.

DON: Your sister told me, that Roberta was 'volatile'.

RICHARD: Yes. It's what I love about her. There's passion. There's energy. She throws herself headlong into life.

DON: Can you tell me a little more about this er… volatility?

RICHARD: Don't do the psychologist bit on me, Dad. You're not the school counsellor anymore. She is perfectly normal but when she feels something she feels it strongly which is what I love about her.

DON: Son, words like volatile worry me. Are you sure you know what you're getting into?

RICHARD: Mum, Dad. Listen to me for once. My life has changed profoundly. My heart tells me there's no turning back.

KATH: Your heart or your penis?

RICHARD: Don't just reduce it to that.

KATH: Sounds like it's a bloody big part of it.

RICHARD: It's a bloody big part of life! My marriage has been without real passion for so long I can't remember.

KATH: If you had any brains left you'd go back to Tracy tonight while she'll still have you. You torture her for much longer and you'll take her past the point where she can forgive.

DON: Your mother's right.

KATH: Your father walked out on me and I tell you if he'd stayed away one day longer I'd have never ever've had him back. The hurt would've been just too great.

DON: [*defending himself*] I was back home again in a week.

KATH: You humiliated me. If I had my life again I wouldn't have taken you back.

DON: And I wouldn't have come back. You paid me out for years afterwards.

RICHARD: You think it was an easy decision for me to take, Mum? Do you think that I enjoy hurting Tracy?

KATH: This Roberta knew what she was doing. She knew you were married.

RICHARD: I seduced her.

KATH: Rubbish. What is she? An artist?

RICHARD: Her work's fantastic.

KATH: Does she sell any?

RICHARD: She's on the cutting edge. She's not commercial.

KATH: And you believe that?

RICHARD: I've seen her work. You haven't.

KATH: Thank God. Wake up, son. She knew what she wanted. A wealthy high status man because she can't earn anything herself. And to hell with the wreckage she caused.

RICHARD: I made the first move.

KATH: Don't you know *anything* about women? Men *never* make the first move. They just think they do.

RICHARD: Mum, will you get this into your head. This is irreversible. I am totally crazy about Roberta and you'll either have to disown me, or live with it. [*His mobile rings. He whips it out. Into the phone*] No, I am not with her! I'm at my parents. Telling Belle. [*He listens, frowning*] No, I'm not going back to her. [*He listens.*] I had to go and check on her. For Christ's sake, she tried to kill herself. [*He listens, frowning.*] Yes of course it was attention seeking, but I had to go and make sure. No, I am not going back to her. Just rest easy, will you? I've got to break the news to Belle and I'll come over later. Roberta, stop yelling. I have to talk to my daughter. I'll be over later.

He switches off the mobile and puts it back in his pocket.

DON: Volatile? Jesus.

RICHARD: Okay! She's being put through the wringer too.

BELLE *appears from the video room.*

BELLE: What are you doing here?

RICHARD: Your mother…

BELLE: What?

RICHARD: She's fine.

BELLE: [*scared*] What's happened?

RICHARD: It's alright, love. It really is.

BELLE: What's happened?

DON: She took some pills but she's fine.

BELLE: Oh God, no!

RICHARD: She's fine.

BELLE: Fine? She just tried to kill herself and she's fine?

RICHARD: She didn't try and kill herself. She rang me as soon as she took the pills.

BELLE: [*distressed, to* RICHARD] I want to see her!

RICHARD: She's asleep and the psychiatrist said not to wake her.

BELLE: I want to go!

RICHARD: I'll be going back there in a minute and when she wakes up I'll come and get you.

BELLE: I want to go now.

RICHARD: Look, this is horrible for you and horrible for me. But truly, she's going to be fine.

BELLE: Granny, will you take me? She needs to know that someone loves her.

KATH: I'm sure she knows that already, Belle. But if it'd make you feel better, sure.

RICHARD: Mum, the psychiatrist said she needs to sleep. [*To* BELLE] If she does wake up I'll come and get you.

BELLE: I'm not going with *you*.

KATH: Belle, when she wakes up Richard can ring me and I'll take you, okay?

> BELLE *storms back offstage.* RICHARD *goes to follow her but his mobile goes again.*

RICHARD: [*into the phone*] Roberta? I didn't hang up on you. No, I am not going back to my wife. Stop shouting! No, I am not coming right away. Yes, of course I'm going back to the hospital. Yes, I know she did it to put pressure on me to come back. That doesn't mean I'm going back. Roberta, listen—

> *She's hung up on him.* RICHARD *is in despair.*

Tracy tries to kill herself. Belle won't speak to me and now Roberta says it's all over with us. What is it with women? They're all fucking crazy.

> *He slumps on the sofa.* MAL *comes out of the video room.*

MAL: Those teen vampire movies. I just don't get it. Something up?

DON: Mal, will you leave us be for a minute.

This only makes MAL *more intrigued to see what's going on.* KATH
sits beside her son and puts her arms around him.

KATH: [*to* RICHARD] Calm down. It'll sort itself out in the long run.

RICHARD: Ten years? Twenty years? I may as well take those fucking
pills myself.

DON: Jesus, son. Don't talk like that. You're scaring the shit out've me.

RICHARD: I'm a fuck-up. I'm a total fuck-up! Wealthy and successful?
Hah! All I do is manipulate poor bastards to buy things they don't
need, that put 'em in debt and don't make them one jot happier…

KATH: You're being too hard on yourself.

RICHARD: [*ranting*] I'm being too soft on myself. You and Dad have
spent your life doing something useful. What have I done? Encourage
people's basest instincts. I tell 'em that if they buy a shiny new
Mercedes everyone's going to envy them, which will make them
incredibly happy. You know what studies show—

DON: You keep the economy growing. You keep people employed.

MAL: Don, that's crap. Economic growth is killing the planet.

DON: Mal, shut up!

RICHARD: Two weeks after they've bought their bloody Mercedes they're
no happier than they ever were. Their little blip of happiness, their
little blip of feeling better than their neighbours has disappeared.

MAL: Of course it has. We're hardwired to never ever be satisfied. A guy's
got three billion, he wants six billion. We're just a mob of insatiably
greedy pricks heading to a grisly end of our own making.

DON: Mal, just shut up.

RICHARD: He's right! I'm making a fortune selling short-term happiness
that leads to long-term disaster.

MAL: Go for it, mate. Sell your shit. Bring on doomsday!

DON: Mal, shut up!

RICHARD: We've got a happy marriage, a lovely son and daughter,
and what happens? We want more. More sex, more glamour, more
excitement, and we fuck up everything.

MAL: It's not your fault, mate. Males are hardwired to root anything
that moves. Spread their genes.

KATH: Mal!

MAL: [*pouring himself another drink*] Nobody wants to hear the truth, mate. Nobody. [*He indicates the video room and, speaking to no-one in particular*] Apparently werewolves and vampires are mortal enemies.

> *He's heading back towards the video room when the doorbell rings.*

I bet I know who that is.

> *He veers off towards the door and opens it.* COOLEY, *smartly but conservatively dressed, and his wife* HELEN, *a little younger than he is, very well dressed, and still very beautiful, accompanies him.*

I knew. I knew. Cooley!

COOLEY: Didn't I go to your funeral?

MAL: That was Mack. Helen, you're looking so… good. Why are you still with him?

HELEN: God knows. He gets more and more set in his ways every year. He re-parked the car three times because it wasn't quite square with the kerb.

> HELEN *is carting a cylinder on wheels behind her.*

MAL: What's that?

HELEN: His oxygen tank. Just in case.

MAL: [*delighted*] Oxygen tank?

HELEN: His emphysema's getting worse and he's bound to get excited tonight.

COOLEY: So what's happening? Are that crappy Labor lot consigned to the dustbin of history where they deserve to be?

MAL: You were a progressive once.

COOLEY: I did think of voting Labor in 1969 but thank God I didn't. Don, Kath! [*He sees* RICHARD, *still distressed*] Richard?

KATH: His marriage is in trouble.

COOLEY: All marriages are in trouble.

> *They exchange handshakes and stand around awkwardly.*

RICHARD: Sorry. I've just fucked up big time. I'll go.

DON: Where?

RICHARD: I just need to drive. With any luck I'll hit a tree and solve everything.

DON: [*agitated*] How do you think your mother and I are going to cope if anything happens to you? Just don't talk like that!

RICHARD: I'm just a fuck-up. I'm no use to anyone.

He gets up to go. KATH *stands in his way.*

KATH: Richard, you're not going anywhere. Give me your car keys.

RICHARD: No!

KATH: Give them to me. Now!

RICHARD fumbles reluctantly in his pocket and hands them over.

Go into the spare room and just lie down. [*She fixes him with an authoritative mother's stare.*] In there! If the hospital rings I'll go in with you.

RICHARD: I'll sort out my own life.

KATH: You've clearly shown you can't. Now get in there and lie down. Don, go to the medicine cabinet. There are some night-time flu capsules.

RICHARD: I haven't got flu.

KATH: They've got sedatives in them. They'll calm you down.

RICHARD: Mum, I'm bloody forty-two.

KATH: Richard, you're scaring the hell out of us. Just do what you're told. Don, take him and give him those tablets.

DON and RICHARD exit, RICHARD *still distressed with DON's comforting arm around his shoulder.*

HELEN: We should go.

KATH: No, please. This is one of those nights I need a few old friends around. What a lovely dress.

COOLEY: [*indicating the absent RICHARD*] Kath, I'm really sorry. When our Greta's arsehole of a husband left her for a grasping young airhead I wanted to kill him. [*He realises what he's said.*] Sorry, I didn't mean— Richard's marriage has probably failed for very good reasons.

KATH: No. Exactly the same.

HELEN: I really do think we should go.

KATH: No really, it's fine. That's a lovely dress, Helen.

HELEN: Oh, it's nothing special.

COOLEY: Nothing special?

HELEN: I bought it at a sale. It was reduced.

COOLEY: From insane to merely outrageous.

KATH: [*to* HELEN] It's not fair. You never damn well age.

HELEN: I was going to say the same about you.

KATH: If you did you'd be lying.

COOLEY: Kath, she's right. You're looking great. Mal, you're looking like shit.

MAL: At least I'm not on oxygen.

COOLEY: Still can't find yourself a woman?

MAL: I've lived by myself for ten years now, mate, and I've never been happier.

COOLEY: Kept the local massage parlour solvent I hear.

HELEN: Grainger! [*To* KATH] He's a perfect gentleman to the point of being boring, except when he meets his old friends.

KATH: We're going to have to listen to the same old stories, most of which never happened.

COOLEY: Enough of them did.

HELEN: Well, we especially don't want to hear those.

KATH: I have a feeling you're going to be disappointed. Would you like something to drink?

COOLEY: What the hell. Pour me a red.

HELEN: Pour him a mineral water.

COOLEY: Honey!

HELEN: You know damn well what the doctor said.

COOLEY: Just half a glass.

HELEN: Mineral water.

KATH *pours him a glass.* COOLEY *takes it reluctantly.*

MAL: What a wuss.

COOLEY: Let's have some music, for God's sake.

He takes his iPod out and puts it on an iPod player. The Creedence Clearwater Revival track 'Bad Moon Rising' blares out and COOLEY *starts to dance, indicating to* KATH *that she join him, an offer she declines. After a while he starts to pant and wheeze.* HELEN *switches the track off and points to the oxygen tank.*

HELEN: Have some of that and don't be so bloody stupid again.

He flops down in a chair. She puts a mask over his face and turns on the oxygen. He gasps and still manages to talk.

COOLEY: You don't need to turn off the music.

HELEN: Creedence Clearwater Revival? It's all you ever play.

COOLEY: Why not? Greatest band of all time.

He takes some more oxygen, then gets up and turns the music on again, gyrating defiantly before he returns to gulp some more oxygen.

HELEN: Alright. Don't listen. End up in hospital.

COOLEY: Find a coffin and lay in it? Miffy, this is a bloody party.

HELEN: Don't call me Miffy!

COOLEY: Well, I have been for thirty-five years.

HELEN: Not in public.

DON *reappears and hears Creedence Clearwater. He starts to gyrate.*

DON: Greatest band ever. You got, 'Who'll Stop the Rain'?

COOLEY: Sure have, mate.

KATH: How's Richard?

DON: He's taken the pills. He's lying down.

KATH *goes to check for herself.* COOLEY *finds 'Who'll Stop the Rain' and turns it up loud. The women wince as the men sing the words, badly and slightly out of tune. They almost get orgasmic when they howl the line. 'Who'll stop the rain'.* BELLE *comes out.*

BELLE: Any news from the hospital?

DON: They're going to call.

MAL: [*to* BELLE] You like Creedence Clearwater?

BELLE: They're in again.

She starts to dance with calculated foxy sexiness. COOLEY *stares.*

COOLEY: Who's this?

DON: Our granddaughter Belle.

COOLEY: Migod. [*To* DON] Thank God she missed out on your genes.

He tries to dance with her but starts coughing and has to retreat to the oxygen again.

HELEN: Grainger, don't make an absolute fool of yourself.

She turns down the music.

BELLE: [*to* COOLEY] Are you Cooley?

COOLEY: Yes I am, m'am.

BELLE: Grandma told me about you.

COOLEY: Nothing bad I hope.

BELLE: She said you used to walk up to women you didn't even know and ask them for sex?

COOLEY: Only if their eyes said, 'Take me, you gorgeous hunk'.

BELLE: That is really so… uncool.

COOLEY: Baby, I was too hot to be cool.

HELEN: Belle, don't listen to him. He's full of bullshit.

COOLEY: Belle, there was a time that when I walked into a room, every female there would feel a rush of blood.

MAL: A wave of nausea.

BELLE: You look like a boring accountant to me.

HELEN: He's a boring lawyer.

COOLEY *catches sight of the television.*

COOLEY: Bloody Kerry O'Brien. Even his left *ear's* bigger than his right.

DON: You want Abbott as our prime minister?

COOLEY: Better than a red-headed sheila with a beak like a Woody Woodpecker. At least Kristina Keneally is rootable.

DON: You want our country to be led by someone who says global warming is bullshit?

COOLEY: It is. Work hard, buy a car or two, and we're supposed to feel guilty about it. It's all crap. It's just a leftist way to try and destroy western enterprise culture.

BELLE: Are you joking?

DON: Sadly he's not.

BELLE: It's alright for you. By the time the really bad stuff happens you'll be dead.

MAL: Hopefully before the end of the night.

BELLE: [*to* COOLEY] You think you know better than thousands of scientists?

DON: Yes he does. Oil's running out. Coal is frying us. Wind and solar can never take up the slack. Uranium is limited. The world is fucked. But who cares? Party on.

BELLE: Granddad, that's just so typical of your generation.

MAL: Belle, our generation gave the warnings. We pointed out just how hollow rampant materialism was. We pointed out how much richer in human terms communal co-operation is to extreme individualism. But the next generations didn't listen. They marched to the tune of greed and the world is facing the consequences.

BELLE: Your generation gave the warnings? I've just finished a big school project on this. Your generation was the greediest, most materialistic, most environmentally destructive generation in the history of the world.

MAL: Now just a—[minute.]

BELLE: You were so busy grabbing what you could get that you couldn't even be bothered having children, which means that all of you are going to have to be supported in your old age by far too few of us. And you've become rich by sitting in houses you bought dirt cheaply, and watching them grow in value to the point where our generation can never afford them.

DON: Now, Belle—

BELLE: Granddad, how much did you pay for this house?

DON: It was forty years ago.

BELLE: How much did you pay for it?

DON: Fourteen thousand, but—

BELLE: How much is it worth now? Seven hundred and fifty thousand? At least?

DON: We've improved it. And inflation—

BELLE: That's over five thousand per cent. That's way, way over inflation. Granddad, you've got rich just by sitting here on your bum. How is that fair?

DON: You're right, we've been lucky, but—

BELLE: You helped yourself to everything you wanted. Oil that took billions of years to create, guzzled and gone in thirty more years.

DON: Belle, our generation is far more aware of the limited nature of our resources.

BELLE: [*pointing*] So how come you've still got two cars out in the driveway? You talk the talk, Granddad, but you don't walk the walk.

MAL: Belle, I still say that our generation was the first to sound the warnings.

BELLE: How come you didn't listen to them?

> KATH *comes back into the room.*

DON: How is he?

KATH: Sleeping. Sort of. He's a mess.

BELLE: He's a mess? He caused the mess!

KATH: [*to* BELLE, *holding up a mobile*] I've got his mobile. The hospital is going to ring when she wakes up. Then we'll all go.

> BELLE *nods and moves off towards the video room.* MAL *watches her go.*

MAL: My God. Some poor bastard's going to be married to that one day.

> *There's a silence.* DON *flicks off the mute and we hear the television.*

KERRY O'BRIEN: [*TV, voice only*] Very early days yet and only a handful of booths but you'd have to say there seems to be a swing on in Queensland and New South Wales. Antony?

ANTONY GREEN: [*TV, voice only*] Yes, early figures but we are seeing quite a swing at this stage.

DON: [*switching the mute on again*] Here we go. Thanks, Queensland. Tomorrow you can all squeeze your beer bellies behind the wheel of your four-wheeled drives and go huntin', fishin' and shootin' knowing Tony will stop the boats and all will be well with the world.

COOLEY: And all the inner-city poofters can have a bit of a cry over their latte and croissants because they won't be able to get married for at least another three years.

The doorbell rings. DON *moves to it as* KATH *comes back into the room.*

DON: Who in the hell is this?

MAL: Jenny.

COOLEY: Jenny?

DON goes to the door and opens it. It's JENNY, MAL*'s ex wife, standing there, looking as formidable as ever.*

DON: Jenny, come in.

KATH: Would you like a drink?

JENNY: Just water, thanks.

JENNY looks at COOLEY *and* HELEN.

COOLEY: Been a while, Jenny.

JENNY: I wonder why that is, Grainger?

COOLEY: It was so long ago. Give me a break.

KATH: We thought you'd be watching the elections with your State Parliament colleagues.

JENNY: [*looking at* MAL] You haven't told them?

MAL: Of course not. I value my life.

JENNY: I've been dumped from Cabinet.

DON: [*puzzled*] From all reports you've been a very good minister.

JENNY: And I'm most likely going to lose preselection for the next State election.

KATH: Why?

JENNY: Because I have this stupid habit of telling the truth. I told Brumby that it's no wonder people are voting for the Greens because the Labor Party has abandoned all of its principles.

DON: Wouldn't go down all that well.

JENNY: [*ferociously*] Well, it's true.

DON: [*quick to placate*] I know it's true. I know it's true.

COOLEY: Bullshit it's true. The Greens want to turn the clock back to the Stone Age and the Labor Party is at least sensible enough to know they can't go down that road.

JENNY: [*bitingly*] What road exactly should they be going down, Grainger? Postponing action on emissions forever? Cheering at the fact that one in ten Australians live in poverty? That one in eight families have to go without meals to pay rents?

COOLEY: Jenny, there are always going to be winners and losers in every society. In fact we need winners and losers to try and motivate the slack-arse losers to become winners.

JENNY: Did you just say what I think I heard you say?

COOLEY: That's what I believe. And I'm allowed to. You lefties are all just a pack of bloody self-righteous bullies.

JENNY: I can't believe I ever... [*shuddering*] it's too horrible to think about.

HELEN: Jenny, let's not bring that all up.

COOLEY: It was thirty-five years ago, for Christ's sake. We were young and stupid and crazy for sex.

JENNY: You were crazy for sex.

HELEN: And so was your husband.

JENNY: My ex husband. He was even more feeble-brained than Grainger.

COOLEY: That's the first compliment you've ever paid me.

JENNY: There won't be any more. Believe me.

COOLEY: I believe you.

JENNY: Don't try and tell me it didn't leave you with scars, Helen.

HELEN: Jenny, it's a long while ago. He's been a great husband, a great father to our kids, and he's never, never looked sideways at another woman since.

KATH: More than I can say about Don.

DON: What is this? Ancient grievance night?

> BELLE *reappears to get something to nibble on from the table. They don't notice her.*

KATH: You betrayed me and it's rather hard to forget.

DON: Elephants have long memories? Not compared to women born in Melbourne. Give me a break. Since then I've been world's best practice husband.

BELLE: What did he do, Grandma?

KATH: [*before she can stop herself*] Ran off with one of his students.

DON: Kath!

KATH: It's time she knew. Gave her psychological counselling and a few years later he's in bed with her.

MAL: Mate, that's not on.

BELLE: It's disgusting.

DON: Belle, she'd left school years before and it was only a matter of days before I realised it wasn't right.

KATH: A week. It was a week.

MAL: Kath, I have to say frankly that I was amazed when you took him back.

DON: [*to* MAL] You sanctimonious arsehole!

KATH: I shouldn't have taken him back.

DON: I made a mistake, Belle. But no matter how many mea culpas I do, the retribution goes on and on and on.

KATH: Because the hurt goes on and on and on.

BELLE: Why'd you stay together?

KATH: Because I'm stupid and weak.

BELLE: I'll tell you one thing. After tonight I don't think I'm ever going to get married.

MAL: That'll save some poor guy a lot of pain.

> BELLE *gives him a withering look and retreats towards her room again. There's an awkward silence.*

JENNY: Excuse me, but I can't help feeling I'm not exactly welcome here.

KATH: When people haven't communicated at all for thirty-five years it's just… a bit… of a shock for them to suddenly… reappear.

JENNY: Everyone's life has unfinished business, Kath.

> BELLE, *having stopped to pick up another bit of food, is almost offstage but this sounds interesting. Although they all assume she's gone, she keeps herself within listening distance.*

DON: [*to* JENNY] It's about the book, right?

JENNY: Yes, it's about the book.

MAL: That book hurt, mate. And it hurt Jenny more than me.

JENNY: You just shut up. I can do my own talking. [*To* DON] I should have said this years ago. Your depiction of me…

DON: It was largely fictional.

JENNY: It was a ruthless betrayal of trust in the interests of your greater glory, which thankfully backfired because the book was so bloody mediocre. And the one thing it was not, was fictional. I was depicted as a whiny, self-pitying, victim of a loveless marriage, who couldn't see any exit and wasn't going to try and find one. That hit me harder than you could ever believe. Even more so because it was true. I went straight down into a very deep well of depression. Have you ever been depressed, Don?

DON: Not till tonight.

JENNY: Well, you wouldn't, would you? Detached Don Henderson. Looking down on our foibles from a great height as if he didn't have any himself. I can't believe you worked as a school counsellor. You don't give a shit.

DON: Whether you want to admit it or not there was a lot of affection and understanding for you all in that book.

JENNY: Well, I'm sorry. The affection went right over my head.

MAL: And mine. Every one of my good points was deliberately left out.

COOLEY: You should've put them in, Don.

MAL: Thank you.

COOLEY: It would've only taken one brief sentence.

DON: Jenny, I heard you got a little down and I was really sorry.

JENNY: A little down? If you ever do get full on depression you'll find it's a lot worse than being a little down. You're in this pit and the sides are slimy and slippery and you try and climb but you just keep sliding down again. Endlessly.

MAL: You caused a lot of damage, mate. A lot of bloody damage.

JENNY: [*to* MAL] Shut up. All you got accused of was having a small prick. Which more than one woman here can vouch for.

MAL: And being obsequious. And insensitive. And a bullshit artist.

COOLEY: Which we can all vouch for.

JENNY: It was the women who got done over in that book. Well and truly.

DON: Nobody read the bloody thing!

JENNY: That wasn't the point. For the first time we realised how you *really* felt about us. You were supposed to be our closest friend. And the way you depicted Kath?

DON: It was sympathetic.

KATH: Sympathetic? Hah! I was a neurotic, pill-popping mess, with scarcely a brain in my head and frigid to boot.

DON: You exaggerate things for dramatic effect.

MAL: You didn't exaggerate the size of my dick.

KATH: Mal's not the only one to be very ordinary in the equipment area, but you depicted yourself as being irresistible to every woman that laid eyes on you.

DON: It's all to do with creating a story structure.

JENNY: I finally dragged myself out of that slimy well, and it took years, Don. Believe me.

DON: Jenny, you can't blame it entirely on me.

JENNY: You were the last straw that tipped me over the edge. The years when I should've been a good mother to my kids I barely had the energy to lift my head.

MAL: You were a great mother.

JENNY: Not during those years, and by God my kids paid a price. You really want to know why I came tonight? I opened the business section of the paper and there was the smiling face of your son Richard under a headline stating that he was one of the most creative brains in Australian advertising. And then the very next day a picture of your lawyer daughter Sadie and her three unbelievably gorgeous children and her banker husband in a lifestyle piece about how a woman can have it all. Wow. I just got so incredibly angry. You guys had the energy to make sure they had every opportunity, while I was right down in that pit that Don had thrown me into.

DON: You can't blame it all on me, Jenny. Your marriage was a mess!

JENNY: And didn't you point that out. Loud and clear.

KATH: Jenny—

JENNY: I didn't manage to have the perfect family, did I? One dead of AIDS, one ex addict, and one lesbian.

DON: Jenny, your son Pete hasn't been using for years. He's making a fortune as a carpenter. And Lucy has a great partner and is getting more work than she can handle as an architect.

MAL: [*to* JENNY] And there's never been anything wrong with Penny. And she's given us two lovely grandchildren. Don't put our bloody kids down.

JENNY: I'd kill for any one of them. But I could've done so much more.

MAL: You were a great mother. Stop bloody torturing yourself!

KATH: From what I hear your grandkids are marvellous.

JENNY: It would have to be from what you hear. You haven't spoken to me for forty years.

KATH: Jenny, our friendship broke down in a fairly acrimonious way *before* Don wrote his book. And Don only communicates with Mal on email. How *could* I see your grandkids?

JENNY: In fact you did me a favour, Don. By the time I'd crawled out of that deep well I was full of fury and determined to prove you wrong.

KATH: It had the same effect on me. It wasn't fun to be depicted as a brainless suburban hausfrau obsessed with her pottery wheel.

DON: You both did brilliantly well, and that's great.

JENNY: It wasn't easy, mate. Juggling an honours degree with four kids isn't fun. But every time I felt like tossing it in I thought of you and the anger surged again. So thank you, Don. You tried to destroy me, but it bloody well failed.

DON: [*angry*] Come on, Jenny! Every writer borrows from life. There's a dictionary of all Charles Dickens' fictional characters and the real-life characters they were based on.

JENNY: If you were as good a writer as Dickens it might be more forgivable.

COOLEY: I've got no complaints. I came across as irresistible to every woman who crossed my path.

DON: As I said, it was a work of fiction.

COOLEY: I *was* a great dick man.

JENNY: You were sex-obsessed to the point of being sick!

COOLEY: [*with a shrug*] Some men just have more red corpuscles.

HELEN: [*to* JENNY] He's not that person anymore.

JENNY: [*to* HELEN] Only because he's on bloody oxygen! How could you have let yourself be a part of all that stupidity?

DON: Can we maybe draw a line under all this? I wrote a lousy novel and as a result you [*indicating* JENNY] became a respected member of State Parliament, and you [*indicating* KATH] became a senior lecturer in art history, so I accept your respective thanks and we can all watch the election unfold.

JENNY: No, I'm not going to just forget that other episode because that totally screwed me up too!

COOLEY: Bloody hell, Jenny. You were right into it. Orgasm after orgasm, then half an hour later out comes the shotgun! You bloody near killed me.

KATH: Shotgun?

JENNY: [*to* COOLEY] I was sucked in and afterwards I felt grubby and ashamed and desperate.

HELEN: You did go over the top, Jenny. It was frightening.

JENNY: [*to* JENNY] Helen, you were freaked out too.

HELEN: I would rather not have done it, but I knew it was just a bit of temporary insanity.

JENNY: Why did you go along with it?

COOLEY: Jesus, a bit of innocent wife swapping. Don and Kath didn't carry on like you, Jenny.

KATH: [*to* COOLEY] You told them what we'd done?

JENNY: Absolutely. Everyone's doing it, was his message.

COOLEY: How could a man not be tempted? You and Kath were really hot back then. And Jenny was the hottest of the lot and half an hour later out comes the shotgun.

JENNY: I meant to miss.

COOLEY: Well, you're not much of a shot. One of the pellets left a hole in my left earlobe.

JENNY: [*pointing to his silver earring*] Don't whinge. You've put it to good use.

KATH: Why did you have a shotgu?

JENNY: To hunt feral cats. [*To* COOLEY] And I never missed one.

HELEN: It was the most terrifying night of my life.

JENNY: [*to* KATH] Didn't you feel enraged?

> *She hesitates, looking at* DON.

KATH: I feel terrible saying this but… no. Cooley was… pretty good.

JENNY: But didn't you feel—

COOLEY: [*interrupting*] And I still am… after a sniff or two of oxygen.

DON: And I was hopeless?

COOLEY: As I remember it there was a slight question around issues of sustainability.

JENNY: [*to* KATH] But didn't you feel degraded afterwards?

KATH: No, exhausted.

COOLEY: Not everyone's a moralistic member of God's police like you.

KATH: Mind you I only wanted to try it once. Helen was so embarrassed the next day she could barely look at either of us.

JENNY: [*to* HELEN] Yet you went on and did it again?

HELEN: I honestly didn't know he was going to spring it on you guys.

COOLEY: It only happened twice! And when I felt a pellet of lead go through my ear I knew it wasn't going to happen again.

KATH: Look, it was crazy, but I can't honestly say it's ruined my life.

JENNY: Yes, well what happened to me didn't happen to you.

MAL: Jenny, not this. No.

JENNY: I got pregnant.

COOLEY: What?

JENNY: I had no idea who the father was. I had to have an abortion which was the worst thing I ever had to do.

MAL: We had four kids already.

HELEN: Oh migod, Jenny. I'm so sorry. I never knew.

> *Tears are suddenly streaming out of* JENNY'*s eyes. Both* KATH *and* HELEN *go to comfort her.*

JENNY: I still feel terrible. I still have dreams. She's four or five and running towards me. She looks the same every time.

MAL: You couldn't have coped with another.

JENNY: I should've had her. I wanted to have her. But you said no. You didn't just say no, you yelled no. You yelled and yelled.

MAL: It mightn't have been mine!

JENNY: Who cares? There's not much to pick between the quality, or lack of it, of your genes or his.

COOLEY: The compliments are really flying tonight.

MAL: We couldn't have had another.

JENNY: My mother had seven! This would've been one who didn't die of AIDS, who didn't almost fall to drugs, but your pathetic male pride made you tell no.

MAL: [*pointing at* COOLEY] Can you imagine me bringing up one of his kids? Total nightmare.

HELEN: [*troubled*] The baby, Jenny. I didn't know about the baby. That's awful.

JENNY: It was. It still is.

COOLEY: Alright. I'm the villain. Go and get your shotgun again and do the job properly this time.

> JENNY *sobs again, still being comforted by* KATH *and* HELEN. KATH *catches* BELLE *staring at them.*

KATH: Belle? Did you hear any of that?

> BELLE *stands there stunned, then manages to nod.*

DON: Belle, they were different times.

> BELLE *turns and goes back towards the video room.* KATH *hurries after her.*

KATH: Belle, just let me explain.

> BELLE *turns on her.*

BELLE: What is there to explain?

KATH: In your life there are always times you behave like an idiot.

BELLE: You enjoyed it? With *Cooley*!

She storms off. KATH *sighs and shrugs.*

KATH: I'll talk to her later.

MAL: [*with a shrug*] Tell her that it's part of being human. We were designed to be promiscuous. The size of our balls relative to our body weight is someone between the wildly promiscuous chimps and the monogamous gorillas.

KATH: That will really convince her.

COOLEY: I've never worked out how the simple act of putting your old fella into the place it's designed to go, can lead to shit that's still there all this time later.

JENNY: Cooley—

COOLEY: Well, okay. Men and sex. It's a problem. But take sex out of the equation and we're pretty reasonable creatures.

MAL: And we've all been good fathers. [*To* JENNY] I was there for Stephen just as much as you were.

KATH: [*to* JENNY] We heard about Stephen. We were so sorry.

JENNY: Not sorry enough to pick up the phone and talk to me.

KATH: I'm sorry. I still feel awful over that.

JENNY: Not that it would've helped. I felt like screaming when someone said to me, 'I know what you must be going through'. No-one who didn't have a kid of their own dying in front of their eyes knew what I was going through.

KATH: I still should have rung.

HELEN: Me too.

COOLEY: We kept picking up the phone but didn't know what to say.

JENNY: I'm sorry to have unloaded all of this, but it's been festering too long.

DON: There was a lot of love between us once. There really was. Try and remember that.

There's a silence. DON *picks up the television mute and turns it on. Everyone retreats to a sofa or chair to watch.*

KERRY O'BRIEN: [*TV, voice only*] Okay, now Antony?

ANTONY GREEN: [*TV, voice only*] Just to say I'm looking at overall figures. I've got Labor losing six seats to the Coalition.

DON *and* MAL *groan.* COOLEY *cheers.*

I've got the Coalition ahead in thirteen other seats which brings you to nineteen. I've got Labor gaining one seat in McEwen and ahead in La Trobe.

MAL: Thank God for Victorian political sanity!

ANTONY GREEN: [*TV, voice only*] At this stage there's a net shift of seventeen seats,

COOLEY: We've won!

ANTONY GREEN: [*TV, voice only*] Now that's still too close to call because some of those seats are doubtful. You don't give them away at this stage of night, but that means that at this stage we'll be here for a long night.

DON *switches off the mute.*

COOLEY: Leave it on. I want to hear Nick Minchin.

DON *throws him the control and gets up.*

DON: [*to* KATH] I'll go and check on Richard.

KATH: I'll come too.

They exit the stage.

MAL: [*to* JENNY] Well, you've really unburdened yourself tonight.

JENNY: I feel a hell of a lot better.

MAL: No-one else does.

MAL *gets up to go in the direction of the video room.*

JENNY: Where are you going?

MAL: To see a vampire movie. It's better than this shit.

JENNY: [*to* HELEN] Do you share your husband's political views?

HELEN: No.

COOLEY: She votes for those lunatic Greens. Unbelievable.

COOLEY *turns on the sound.*

NICK MINCHIN: [*TV, voice only*] I agree with Antony that it's going to be a long night, but I must say, looking at the swing in Queensland of five point eight per cent on the ten per cent counted, if it's uniform we'll pick up ten seats.

KERRY O'BRIEN: [*TV, voice only*] If it's uniform.

NICK MINCHIN: [*TV, voice only*] If it's uniform. We just don't know that and we won't know that for a while.

COOLEY: [*turning the sound down*] Nick, you're a true warrior of the Right. Why did you resign?

JENNY: Are trying to provoke me, Grainger. Because, by God, if you want a fight you'll get one.

COOLEY: [*shaking his head sadly*] Jenny, Jenny. You were so hot.

JENNY: [*warning*] I've still got the gun.

> JENNY *turns to go to the bathroom.* COOLEY *turns morosely to* HELEN.

COOLEY: Why did you drag me along here with these losers?

HELEN: They were part of our lives, Grainger. A big part.

COOLEY: We were invited to the Jeffersons. There would've been no-one there with a net worth smaller than twenty million.

HELEN: The past means something. It does to me.

COOLEY: I haven't met a Labor voter for twenty years. It's a psychic shock to have to mix with idiots again.

HELEN: You've been emailing these guys for years.

COOLEY: Yes, but only about the football.

HELEN: I like being somewhere where you're allowed to suggest that the world is headed in a seriously dangerous direction. Not have to listen to people with outrageous carbon footprints endlessly congratulating themselves on their success.

COOLEY: [*defiantly*] Well, I still say Nick Minchin is a bloody hero.

> HELEN *looks at him witheringly. He goes back to watching the screen.*
>
> *The lights fade.*

END OF ACT ONE

ACT TWO

It's much later in the night. All of the guests are by now back watching the events on the television unfold. Some are sitting, some are standing. The tension of the cliffhanger night is showing. MAL *in particular has had more to drink.*

KERRY O'BRIEN: [*TV, voice only*] Maxine McKew joins me from Bennelong. Maxine, you've got a place in history as the second person to take a seat from a sitting prime minister, but you've lasted one term. How are you feeling about this right now?

MAL: How the hell do you think she's feeling about it!

COOLEY: You can't just parachute a media personality into a seat and think you've got it sewn up forever.

DON: The Liberals just parachuted a tennis star in there.

MAL: Did you see that disgusting news clip where he's teaching Tony Abbott to hit the ball back over the net? That's a skill that's really going to help him run the country.

KATH: Mal, will you just shut up. We want to hear what she's saying!

MAXINE MCKEW: [*TV, voice only*] Kerry, there are some very big questions for the Labor Party given what has happened tonight.

COOLEY: Yeah, like why do you let a handful of faceless men make all the decisions behind the scenes?

JENNY: Oh, God. Not that old chestnut.

COOLEY: Assassins at midnight. Took an elected prime minister and cut his throat before any of his elected colleagues knew it. That's democracy?

DON: You emailed me a few months ago and said something like, 'Kevin Rudd is a hopelessly dysfunctional little control freak creep, who shouldn't be running a school canteen, let alone a nation'.

COOLEY: Yeah, but the faceless assassins at midnight. It's un-Australian, mate.

DON: And how did Tony Abbott get to be leader? Turnbull just had a few seconds more warning before the knife hit his back.

COOLEY: Australians will not tolerate faceless assassins at midnight.

KATH: Can we please listen to Maxine?

MAL: Cooley, all you've got to learn is 'Great big new tax', 'We'll stop the boats' and 'Spending like drunken sailors', and you'll have Abbott's complete repertoire.

COOLEY: What about Gillard's 'Move Australia forward'? She said it twenty-eight times in one speech.

ALL THE WOMEN: Can we please listen to Maxine!

They shut up.

MAXINE MCKEW: [*TV, voice only*] When we walked away from the prosecution of the CPRS, that cut through here immediately. People saw it as a core belief issue. 'Well look, you argued for this. You said it was the most important thing. And if you walk away from that, what else are you going to walk away from?' So I have to say the disappointment with the kind of government we said we would be has been acute.

JENNY: And who convinced Rudd to drop it? Julia Gillard!

KATH: Be fair to her. We can't act before the rest of the world.

JENNY: We're the world's biggest per capita polluters. We have a moral duty to act.

DON: Whatever happened to political courage? Keating went to Redfern and told Australians they'd behaved like bastards to our indigenous people. No votes in that. He just happened to *believe* in it! Now the whole Labor Party policy is crafted to pander to focus groups of racist bogans in western Sydney who think a handful of wretched refugees are about to erect a mosque in their backyard.

JENNY: And Julia fell over backwards to be as tough on refugees as Abbott.

KATH: There's a huge irrational fear of the boat people out there. Julia has to take that into account.

JENNY: Why? I'm with Don. Why not for once show some political courage? Instead of cowering in the corner and pandering to racists, she might have actually got some respect. I know you're thrilled we have a female prime minister, Kath, but—

KATH: It's not that. The Greens are pushing her from the left and the blue collar voters from the right. She's in a very difficult situation.

HELEN: She should show more courage. Most of those boat people are absolutely desperate.

COOLEY: Let them join the queue.

JENNY: [*ferociously*] In Afghanistan? There isn't a bloody queue, you insufferable dickhead. Their only crime is that they're Muslim.

HELEN: I can't believe there are so many Australians who are just plain intolerant.

JENNY: If we had a policy of deporting Hillsong members that'd make far more sense.

DON: In all fairness, Jenny, all religions are a load of medieval horseshit, but the Muslim religion is right up there amongst the worst.

MAL: Moralistic, rigid, puritanical, profoundly sexist and endorsing huge levels of hatred against anyone who's not one of them.

COOLEY: [*to* MAL] So you'll be down there when the boats arrive saying, 'You're moralistic, rigid, puritanical and profoundly sexist. Welcome to Australia.'

DON: I was just making a point about religion in general.

COOLEY: No you weren't, you left-wing wanker. You were saying you hate Muslims as much as anyone who voted for Pauline Hansen.

MAL: That wasn't what we were saying.

DON: We were speaking about extremist Muslims.

COOLEY: I'm sorry, I missed that word extremist. You guys are the pits. You spout all your progressive bullshit and it's all just words. My wife doesn't get up on a soapbox, but she actually does something.

HELEN: Leave me out of it.

COOLEY: Miffy, your whole life is spent worrying about the poor and the underprivileged. It drives me crazy. I got an hour lecture the other night about the fact that food prices are rocketing and that the world's poor are suffering low-level starvation. What can I do about it? What can you do about it?

HELEN: Quite a bit more than we're doing.

COOLEY: We're already paying a fortune to Care Australia, and God knows what other bloody mob. We're supporting about ten thousand Third World children and digging ten thousand freshwater wells and buying five thousand goats and pigs.

MAL: Helen, sorry. It's just shuffling the deckchairs on the *Titanic*.

HELEN: [*upset*] No it's not! There are doctors, nurses and aid workers working for next to nothing in incredibly risky places to help people with real problems. Not agonising about when they will be able to afford that jet ski!

KATH: [*putting her arm around* HELEN] Let's go and watch in the other room. I'm sick of having to listen to these loudmouths.

COOLEY: Speak your opinion and you're an insufferable dickhead.

HELEN *nods gratefully. She wants to get away from them all for a while.*

HELEN: Isn't young Belle in there watching videos?

KATH: Young Belle has locked herself in the spare bedroom.

DON: Oh, God.

KATH: She'll calm down. I'll talk to her later.

DON: Is Richard okay?

KATH: Last time I looked in he was sleeping.

KATH *and* HELEN *start to move off.* JENNY *gets up to follow them.*

JENNY: [*to* KATH, *conciliatory*] Look, however bitter I am, I still prefer Julia to Tony Abbott.

KATH: Jenny, if you didn't, I'm afraid I'd have to ask you to leave.

They go offstage. DON *stands and watches them go.*

MAL: Helen really feels stuff, doesn't she?

DON: She always did.

COOLEY: She joined one of those refugee support groups. She was at one of the detention centres when the kids started sewing their lips up.

DON *continues to look offstage. He seems about to follow the three women when* COOLEY *turns up the sound on the TV. It catches his attention.*

KERRY O'BRIEN: [*TV, voice only*] For the first time tonight Antony is calling seventy-three seats for Liberal, seventy-two Labor. Do you have a view on the circumstances of how a minority government is formed?

WAYNE SWAN: [*TV, voice only*] I can't speculate tonight. I think we're just going to have to look at how the figures look over the next day or two.

KERRY O'BRIEN: [*TV, voice only*] Do you acknowledge now that it's virtually impossible for Labor to form government in its own right?

DON: [*pushing the mute button*] Oh migod, it's actually going to happen. Bob Katter's going to be deciding our fate.

MAL: The only man in Australia who can string together three contradictory assertions in the one sentence.

DON: Who are the other independents?

MAL: Tony Windsor and Rob Oakshott.

DON: What do you know about them?

MAL: Windsor's conservative but smart. Oakshott is away with the pixies.

COOLEY: Don't get excited, guys. They're from conservative electorates. If they want to get re-elected there's only one way they can vote.

MAL: They'll vote whichever way keeps them holding the balance of power.

COOLEY: They'll vote with Abbott. The election's over. You got cable?

> DON *nods.* COOLEY *grabs the television control from* DON *and switches the channel to a telecast of an Australian Rules football match.*

COOLEY: Go, Doggies!

DON: Doggies? You're a Cats supporter.

COOLEY: The Doggies are playing Sydney.

MAL: Julia Gillard barracks for the Doggies.

COOLEY: [*remembering, so changing his allegiance*] Go, Sydney!

> DON *and* MAL *watch for a second then go upstage into the kitchen area to pour themselves another red wine, talking to each other as they go.*

DON: Where did the years go, mate? Where did they go?

MAL: Our student days were the best times we ever had.

DON: Each day you woke up and thought something could happen that day which could totally change your life.

MAL: Don't, mate. I get too sad.

DON: A brilliant lecture that could alter the way you saw the world, a radical article in the student paper that would set you on fire, an invitation to a party where you'd meet a beautiful woman who'd find you spellbinding—

MAL: Mate, *that* was never going to happen. You were as boring as batshit.

DON: The street marches against the Vietnam war. Police horses charging at us and us holding our ranks. We had fucking courage and fire and we were right. The Vietnam war was hideous bullshit. We fought, mate. We fought. I loved it. I loved every moment of it. There was purpose. There was idealism. There was selflessness. There was comradeship. There was camaraderie.

MAL: Stop it, mate. You're making me cry.

DON: The anti-nuclear march we went on. Frankston to the the city. Twenty-six miles. Camped overnight. First time I heard Bob Dylan's 'The Times They Are A-Changing'.

MAL: We met Cooley on that march. Even he was a radical back then.

DON: No, I think he'd just heard that the peacenik women were sure-fire lays. [*He sighs.*] I loved you back then, mate. We were foot soldiers together. Brother's in arms. I loved you. You turned out to be a total arsehole, but those old bonds never die.

MAL: How did we fuck up our lives so much?

DON: I didn't fuck mine up as much as you.

MAL: How could it start so brilliantly and go so wrong?

DON: Frankly, mate, and I say this as a friend, you made some pretty poor choices.

MAL: Yeah, I shouldn't have tried to start my own business.

DON: Earlier than that.

MAL: What?

DON: Marrying Jenny. She's got admirable qualities. But God, you must have sensed she was going to be a bloody handful.

MAL: I know what you all thought of Jenny.

DON: We had reason, mate. She was time bomb and she's still ticking.

MAL: Alright, she could be bad-tempered, stubborn and judgemental, but she was a wonderful mother to our kids, and she had fire, mate. She had the guts to go back and finish a degree in political science, then carve out a political career. She was one of the best ministers in the government. And when our Stephen was dying of AIDS she sat by his bed for weeks on end. If she'd have me I'd go back tomorrow. Of all our wives, she's the success story.

DON: [*protesting*] Kath did bloody well too. She got a PhD.

MAL: [*disparaging*] Where from? Deakin?

DON: She became an academic and author.

MAL: [*with a sigh*] We thought we were so brilliant and they were so lucky to have us, but we were the ones who bombed out.

DON: I wouldn't say I—

MAL: We bombed out. You got one mediocre novel published and you suddenly thought you were God's gift to women and waltzed off with some floozy.

DON: I was back again in a week.

MAL: You had a few drinks one day and told me that it was the price Kath had to pay for living with a genius.

DON: [*horrified*] Shit, mate. I would never have said that. Talented maybe, but not genius.

MAL: You did, mate. Believe me. I just wanted to punch your lights out.

DON: I would never have said genius.

MAL: It turns out you were barely even talented.

DON: I got some very good reviews.

MAL: One. The rest said it was a wank.

DON: At least I tried. All you were ever interested in was making money.

MAL: Mate, if you'd grown up dirt poor in a shitty little country town with a father who was a violent drunk and a mother who was too busy keeping out of harm's way to ever give us love, you might understand why I wanted to climb out of all that. And when I did it was great. I could go to any restaurant, throw parties, buy my kids expensive presents, send them to private schools, take out a mortgage on a place in South Yarra, take holidays overseas. It was magic. I was living the dream. And mate, be truthful, you were as envious as all hell.

DON: I'll admit it.

MAL: Which frankly was the icing on the cake.

DON: And then you stuffed it by getting too greedy.

MAL: It all would've been fine if I hadn't made a few mistakes in that prospectus.

DON: Few mistakes? It was totally fraudulent. You deserved to be sent to the slammer.

MAL: At least they put me in one of those middle-class jails. I didn't get buggered. But much to your delight my salad days were over.

DON: Well, you did swagger a lot in those days, mate. [*Beat.*] I wrote four more novels, you know.

MAL: Not published?

DON: Rejected. Every one of them. I wasted ten years trying to prove to myself that I really was a writer. Ten years I could've spent more time with my kids.

MAL: Yeah, kids sense when they aren't really wanted.

DON: They were wanted!

MAL: It leaves scars. Richard's still obviously looking for love.

DON: You really are a great friend, Mal. I open up to you and you do your best to amplify every anxiety I've got.

MAL: I'm a truth-teller, mate. If you want a friend who licks your arse and says you're wonderful, it's not me.

DON: It certainly isn't.

> *He hears the television switch back to the election. He moves towards it.* MAL *follows.*

Back on the election?

COOLEY: It's half-time.

DON: Who's winning?

COOLEY: Sydney ten goals six, Doggies six three.

MAL: Kidding?

COOLEY: Julia's going to have a losing night all round.

DON: [*pointing at figures on the screen*] Seventy-two to seventy-three, mate. It's not over.

COOLEY: It better be. If Gillard gets in she'll start hacking away at my superannuation. I've booked us in for a Danube cruise and a trip to Antarctica next year.

MAL: You might have to fly business class rather than first? You've got real worries, mate.

> RICHARD, *looking angry, emerges from the bedroom.*

RICHARD: Dad!

DON: Just a minute, son, I just want to see where the election's at.

RICHARD: All my life it's been 'just a minute, son'. Forget the bloody election. I went to try and talk to Belle and find she's in a state of semi shock.

> COOLEY *and* MAL *look at each other, realise they're not wanted and slide off towards the kitchen, with* MAL *lingering and trying to catch what's going on.* KATH *hears the raised voice of her son and reappears.*

What have you been telling Belle?

DON: Son, she wasn't meant to hear.

RICHARD: Well, she has heard and now I've heard too. What kind of lives were you leading? All of you sleeping together? In the same bed?

DON: Look, it wasn't as bad as it sounds.

RICHARD: Six of you having group sex together?

KATH: No, just four.

RICHARD: You didn't know whose child it was? Had to have abortions?

KATH: That wasn't us. That was Jenny.

RICHARD: Which four? When? Whose child am I?

KATH: Ours, for heaven's sake. This happened after you and your sister were born.

RICHARD: That's great. Young kids and you start having orgies? You were doing this in this house. When we were here?

DON: No, we went away for a weekend. Your grandmother was looking after you.

RICHARD: So which couple was it?

DON: I don't want to talk about it. It only happened once, it was stupid and we're all ashamed.

KATH: It was ridiculous. And it only happened once.

RICHARD: Mal?

KATH: No!

RICHARD: Cooley?

KATH: You've got to understand the times. It was embarrassing and insignificant.

RICHARD: [*to* KATH] That's not what Belle said. She said you loved it!

KATH: She must've misheard.

RICHARD: She didn't mishear.

KATH: I made sure it never happened again.

RICHARD: [*pointing at his mother accusingly*] How can you be so moralistic about Roberta when you did this sort of stuff?

KATH: Once.

RICHARD: At least I'm in love. At least I've never treated sex like a game!

DON: Son—

RICHARD: Belle's always worshipped you, Mum. What kind of sense is she supposed to make out of life after hearing that?

KATH: A much greater problem for Belle is how you're behaving now, not something I did once thirty-five years ago.

RICHARD: Whatever she feels about me, this hasn't helped. [*To* DON] And you had sex with Helen?

DON: Yes, son. Once.

KATH: What did you think? Your parents were perfect.

RICHARD: Oh, no. I never thought that. Never.

DON: What's that meant to mean?

RICHARD: You might have been great at sorting out the problems of your kids at school but you were never there for me.

DON: What?

RICHARD: Have you any idea of what sort of agonies I went through when I was a kid?

DON: What agonies?

RICHARD: Forget it.

DON: No, if you've got something to say, say it. It seems every other bloody thing is out in the open.

RICHARD: I was depressed for years.

DON: Son, I know the signs of depression very well and you weren't depressed.

RICHARD: Every girl in my form thought I was a dork.

DON: They always think boys their own age are dorks.

RICHARD: The younger ones thought I was a dork too!

KATH: Richard, you were a lovely boy. We were so proud.

DON: Okay, you weren't good at sport and you did have that acne problem and a bit of a stutter, and you hadn't filled out then, but—

RICHARD: I was painfully shy and every day was agony.

DON: Really?

KATH: Of course he was shy. Didn't you even realise he was shy?

RICHARD: [*to his father*] I came home from a school dance one night totally shattered. There was a ladies' choice dance and I was the only one not chosen. I finally plucked up the courage to tell you and all you said was, 'You're lucky. Women will only cause you grief.'

KATH: That's a brilliant bit of psychological counselling!

DON: Hey, listen, I always thought you were a great kid. Sensitive, considerate, bright. I guess your mother and I loved you so much we assumed everyone else did too. I'm sorry.

This simple statement brings tears to RICHARD's *eyes and he impulsively hugs his father who pats his back.*

I'm sorry. I just thought you were so wonderfully sane compared to the kids I was dealing with.

RICHARD: I know, I remember the stories.

DON: Reggie? Total little psychopath. I had to report to the Department every morning whether I thought he was showing signs of being violent that day. Finally murdered his sister. I guess I thought you were perfect by comparison.

They hug each other again.

RICHARD: I've fucked up, Dad. I'm in love with Roberta big-time and now she's thrown me over.

DON: If Roberta can't understand that you have to take care of your wife when she attempts suicide, then believe me this is not someone you should plan on spending your life with.

RICHARD: You don't understand, Dad. She's opened up the possibilities of life to me. I was stuck in a terrible rut, doing a job I hate. All that's over.

KATH: You're tossing in your job?

RICHARD: I can't stay in advertising.

KATH: Richard, you've found something you're very good at, and it earns you very good money and it's highly creative.

RICHARD: To what ends?

KATH: One day when society learns how to keep the economy afloat without advertising then… fine. But that's a long way off, so don't feel the slightest bit guilty about it anymore.

The doorbell rings. DON *looks at* KATH.

DON: Who the hell is that?

KATH shrugs. DON *goes to open the door. A dark, very attractive, sexily-dressed woman of thirty comes in. She's* ROBERTA, *and she's been crying. She sees* RICHARD *and races to him.*

ROBERTA: Dicky, I'm sorry, I'm sorry, I'm sorry.

She throws herself around his neck and embraces him passionately. RICHARD *tries to respond but is embarrassed in front of his parents.*

I am so, so, so sorry.

She hugs him again. By this time MAL *and* COOLEY *are craning their necks in the kitchen to see what's happening.* ROBERTA *turns to* DON *and* KATH.

You're Mr and Mrs Henderson?

They nod, taken aback.

I'm so sorry to intrude, but I had to see him.

RICHARD: How did you find me here?

ROBERTA: You told me they lived near the Lower Plenty pub, so I drove round until I found your car. I'm so sorry. I didn't mean anything I said. Of course you have to go to your wife when she does something like that. I was just desperate I was going to lose you. [*To* KATH *and* DON] I love your son so much. Believe me. It's like an ache. I just got panic-stricken that I might lose him.

RICHARD: [*embarrassed*] Roberta, it's alright. Calm down.

ROBERTA: Is Tracy alright? Is she really alright? I couldn't stand it if I thought I'd caused her any harm.

KATH: [*tersely*] She's very upset.

ROBERTA: But she's alright. Tell me she's alright. I couldn't bear it if she's not alright.

RICHARD: She's alright.

KATH: She's actually not alright. She's sedated in hospital, being closely monitored.

ROBERTA: I'm so sorry. But when you feel like I do, you can't just cut out your heart. And Belle. Little Belle. How's she coping?

KATH: Maybe you should ask her.

RICHARD: Not great.

ROBERTA: I know how hard it must be for her. [*To* KATH *and* DON] I know how hard it must be for you, but please believe I love your son so much. If I didn't I wouldn't be here.

RICHARD: Roberta, let's see if we can calm down a little.

ROBERTA: [*to* KATH *and* DON] I'm sorry. I shouldn't have come but I was half out of my mind. I'm sorry. I'm an emotional person. My mother's Italian. Finally the love of my life appears as if by magic and I can't step back. I know I should but I can't.

RICHARD: Roberta, it's alright. Just calm down.

ROBERTA: [*to* KATH *and* DON] This is not what I wanted. Never what I wanted. I'm not the sort of person who enjoys causing other people pain. If there was any way I could step back I would, believe me. I'm sorry. My mind's racing. I had to come. I know it'll be horrible for you for a while, but I swear I'll make him happy. I swear it's going to be fine in the long run.

KATH: No it isn't. He's got two children and his marriage, until you came on the scene, was perfectly fine.

RICHARD: [*angry*] I'm sorry but you don't dictate the agenda. We love each other and finally that's the only thing that counts.

ROBERTA: I'm sorry. A suicide attempt is horrible. I've tried to kill myself twice and it's horrible. I'm sorry I've caused this. I really am, but I can't give him up.

RICHARD: Roberta, you don't have to give me up. I've explained how I feel to my parents.

ROBERTA: Really? God, I love you. You fight for me and I fight for you. I'm sorry. I'm really off the air at the moment. Please, Mr and Mrs Henderson. I'd die without your son. I really would. I have never, ever loved anyone like I love him in my entire life.

> *She starts to cry.* RICHARD *comforts her.*

RICHARD: [*to* DON *and* KATH] We'll head off. Can I have my car keys back, Mum?

> BELLE *appears from her room, having heard the racket.*

BELLE: What's she doing here?

RICHARD: Belle, we'll talk about this tomorrow.

BELLE: Why did you let her come here?

RICHARD: She found me.

ROBERTA: Belle, I know how you feel right now. But one day, I swear, we will be very, very good friends.

BELLE: Good friends? I'd rather be bosom buddies with a funnel web spider.

RICHARD: Belle! Keep a civil tongue in your head.

BELLE: Good friends?

RICHARD: She said 'one day'. One day when you realise that what I'm doing is real, that what I'm feeling is real.

BELLE: You want to know how long that's going to be? Try never.

ROBERTA: I can understand how you feel, but—

BELLE: No, you can't understand how I feel. If you did you'd be out that door, because I'm this far [*holding up a finger and thumb close together*] from picking up that knife [*pointing to a knife set in the kitchen*] and plunging it into your heart. Except it's probably so small I wouldn't be able to find it.

ROBERTA: [*angry*] Your father's got no right to lead the life he really wants to lead?

BELLE: Roberta, I'm not stupid. I could get any boy at my school to do anything I want him to if he thought there's a chance I'd give him a hand job.

RICHARD: Belle, that's a really revolting thing to say.

BELLE: Revolting people deserve revolting things said to them.

ROBERTA: [*angry*] What's happening between your father and I is far more than just sex.

BELLE: He wants the sex, you want his money!

RICHARD: Belle, go back to the bedroom immediately!

BELLE: You think you've still got some kind of authority over me?

ROBERTA: [*a near hysterical outburst*] It's no use, Richard. It's no use. I can't live with that level of poison. I'd hoped she might at least have tried to understand that if you're very, very lucky in life you find the partner you were always meant to have! I just can't live with that level of viciousness!

KATH: For God's sake, Roberta, don't be so bloody self-centred. Belle's mother is in hospital after a serious attempt on her own life!

RICHARD: Mum!

He puts his arms protectively around ROBERTA. *She breaks free.*

ROBERTA: It's no use, darling. What they don't realise is that I'm even more vulnerable than your wife!

She takes out a bottle of pills and starts stuffing them in her mouth. DON, *who's nearest, snatches them out of her hand and slaps her back, making her cough them up.* ROBERTA *starts wailing and sobbing and falls into* RICHARD's *arms.*

RICHARD: Did you swallow any?

DON: No, she didn't.

RICHARD: How would you know?

DON: Son, I was a counsellor in a school full of lovesick adolescent girls. Two or three might have gone down, but that'll just put her to sleep.

ROBERTA *is still sobbing uncontrollably.*

Take her into the bedroom and keep an eye on her. When she goes to sleep I need to talk to you.

RICHARD *leads her, still sobbing, into the bedroom.* MAL *and* COOLEY *come down from the kitchen and* JENNY *and* HELEN *appear.*

JENNY: What was all that about?

KATH: [*ironically to* JENNY] My son's new girlfriend tried to take an overdose. Just a minor little episode in the life of our wealthy, successful son.

JENNY: Kath—

KATH: Our daughter's marriage is in good shape, so you can maintain your rage on that one.

JENNY: Kath, I'm sorry.

MAL: I can understand why his marriage is in trouble. She is hot!

JENNY: Mal!

MAL: Totally crazy, but hot.

JENNY: You find a woman who takes overdoses attractive?

MAL: Tempestuous turns me on.

COOLEY: Mate, steady up. She's just tried to kill herself.

MAL: It was all for show.

JENNY: What if you were wrong for once in your life!

She turns away from him shaking her head.

BELLE: I hope she dies. I really hope she dies.

KATH: Belle, come here.

KATH *sits on the sofa and indicates that* BELLE *sit beside her. She hesitates but finally does.* HELEN *and* JENNY *move tactfully offstage back to the other television room.*

DON: I'll just go and check on those two.

He leaves. COOLEY *realises that* KATH *wants to be alone with* BELLE *and nudges* MAL.

COOLEY: Come and see my new Merc.

MAL: Why would I want to see your new bloody Merc?

COOLEY: Because it's a masterpiece of German engineering and every now and then you need to be reminded what a total bloody failure you are.

He shoves MAL *towards the back door and they go out.*

KATH: Belle, it's going to be alright.

BELLE *can't sustain the sassy young girl act. She's confused and anxious. Tears form in her eyes and she buries her head into her grandmother's shoulder.*

Truly, it's going to be alright.

BELLE: How? Dad's an idiot. That woman's mad.

KATH: Yes, and your father will get to realise it.

BELLE: When?

KATH: Hopefully sooner rather than later.

BELLE: He says he doesn't love Mum anymore. I don't even think he loves me.

KATH: He certainly loves you.

There's a pause.

I'm sorry you heard all that stuff. [*Beat.*] No, actually I'm not. It's just as well that you know nobody's perfect. Especially not your grandparents.

BELLE: [*screwing up her nose*] How could you watch each other do it?

KATH: You have to understand the times. Australia in the fifties was the most repressed nation on earth. Books were banned if they had sex in them. Then suddenly in the late sixties came the rebellion. Sex was natural, sex was fun. It was mind-blowing. Well, it was until you realised sex *wasn't* a party game. Which in my case didn't take all that long.

BELLE: I've done things with boys, but not…

KATH: [*with a shrug*] Good, because there is something called love. Without it life would be pretty bleak.

BELLE: But you did it with someone you didn't love.

KATH: Yes, but I *was* very fond of Cooley in those days.

BELLE: [*amazed*] Really?

KATH: That's why I didn't do it any more.

BELLE: Cooley?

KATH: He was a terrible chauvinist and still is, but there was a heart there that you could always sense. His sister's boy died of leukaemia and he's raised millions for cancer in the last twenty years.

BELLE: After it happened, did you ever think… you should be with him?

KATH: [*with a shrug*] I had 'what if' fantasies from time to time. Most women do. It stirs up a nice little mood of melancholy now and then.

> BELLE *snuggles closer to her grandmother*

BELLE: They don't teach this sort of stuff in our personal development classes.

KATH: Belle, it's going to be pretty bad for you and your mother. I'm sorry.

> *She gets up off the sofa.* MAL *and* COOLEY *come back inside and* MAL *pours himself another glass of red on the way.* HELEN *comes back in with* JENNY *as* DON *reappears from the bedroom.*

How is she?

DON: She's fine. Took just enough to send her to sleep.

KATH: How's Richard?

DON: Sitting on the bed, holding her hand, muttering I love you, Mimsie, or some other revolting pet name.

> KATH *gets up to go and see him.* DON *shakes his head.*

Leave him alone. He's got to sort this one out himself.

BELLE: She's crazy, isn't she, Granddad?

DON: I think she's got a personality disorder but she's not crazy crazy.

KATH: What disorder?

DON: She's got what they call a histrionic personality. Life is always a drama and if it isn't you turn it into one.

KATH: Why can't Richard see that?

DON: When you're in love all rational mental activity ceases.

KATH: So no matter what we say it'll make no difference?

DON: [*with a shrug*] Not much.

JENNY: Sorry, Kath. I really am.

> KATH *nods.* BELLE *exits with tears in her eyes.* DON *sits himself on the sofa and stares straight ahead.*

KATH: I'm going outside. I need some air.

JENNY: Me too.

KATH: [*as they go*] Have you got any photos of your grandkids?

JENNY: [*reaching for her bag*] I've got a whole gallery full in the back of my Filofax if you can bear it.

> *They let themselves out.* DON *turns up the television.*

KERRY O'BRIEN: [*TV, voice only*] Ah, hang on. We're going to cross to Labor Party headquarters where Julia Gillard is arriving. It's absolutely in the balance whether she becomes the first elected female prime minister in history, but if she does it will be on the basis of a minority government. This has been an absolute roller-coaster ride for Julia Gillard and here she is now.

> *The sound of rather forced chants of 'Julia, Julia' are heard on the television.*

COOLEY: They're really working overtime to try and sound enthusiastic.

MAL: Frankly, and a lot of people don't agree with me, I think she's really horny.

JENNY: Mal!

MAL: She's like the classroom good girl that you want to bend over the desk and liven up.

JULIA GILLARD: [*TV, voice only*] Thank you very, very much. Friends, Bill Clinton once famously said in a previous election in America that the people have spoken, but it's going to take a little while to determine exactly what they've said. And that's where we find ourselves tonight. What we know from tonight's results is that there will be a number of independents in the House of Representatives playing a role as the next Government of Australia is formed. I acknowledge and congratulate Rob Oakshott on his re-election as the member for Lyne, Tony Windsor on his re-election as the member for New England and

Bob Katter on his re-election as the member for Kennedy and the election of Adam Bandt to the seat of Melbourne.

COOLEY: Can you believe that? She's sucking up to them already! With a voice like a crosscut saw. I can't bear it.

> COOLEY *turns the football back on.* DON *protests.*

DON: Watch it in the other room.

COOLEY: Hasn't got cable. Go, Kieran Jack, you bloody little champion.

> DON *looks at* HELEN *and they go towards the other room as* MAL *and* COOLEY *watch the football.* HELEN *stops.*

HELEN: I don't think I want to see any more.

DON: Yeah, it's too depressing. A drink?

HELEN: Yeah, why not.

> DON *takes a bottle and glass from a downstage table and pours her a glass. They sit down on chairs around the dining table at some distance from the television.*
>
> *There's a pause.*

DON: I didn't know you were doing all that refugee work.

HELEN: I saw a report on television about the long-term damage that incarceration was doing to them.

DON: You make me feel really ashamed. I'm a psychologist. I could have helped.

HELEN: You still can. We'll be back to the razor wire compounds no matter who wins tonight.

DON: I will. I mean it. I really will.

> *There's a short silence.* DON *looks around to check nobody is within earshot. Beat.*

I'm still sort of crazy about you, you know.

HELEN: How much have you been drinking?

DON: Enough for me to tell the truth.

HELEN: Don, it was so long ago.

DON: I know. [*Beat.*] I just wanted to let you know.

HELEN: You came up with a pretty exotic cover story. An ex student?

DON: I had myself at a counsellors' conference, but she checked and found I wasn't there. I panicked and that was the best I could come up with. It wasn't very smart. I think it enraged her more than if I'd told the truth. Was Grainger ever suspicious?

HELEN: No, I was on totally safe grounds there. Grainger could never believe that any woman in the world would prefer any other man to him.

DON: Do you regret that week?

HELEN: Don, it was so long ago.

DON: I've kept thinking about it all these years.

HELEN: I do too, but—

DON: I think what if we had've had the guts to go through with it? What would our lives have been like?

HELEN: We didn't go through with it.

DON: I've even thought—

HELEN: What?

DON: Is it too late?

HELEN: Yes, it's far too late.

DON: Yeah. I thought you'd say that.

HELEN: We can't suddenly tell our families, 'Hey, sorry. This last thirty-five years has been a charade.' We couldn't do that even if we wanted to.

DON: Would you want to?

HELEN: Don, the truth is we were never going to go through with it. Two small children each, and two partners who periodically made us tear our hair out, but who we really liked a hell of a lot. It was a great little fantasy, but reality finally bit.

DON: It never quite bit for me.

HELEN: I can't really say my life has been miserable. And if you're honest, neither has yours.

DON: No.

HELEN: I try and look at it philosophically. Every marriage should have one of those weeks somewhere in it, and we were lucky enough to pull it off.

DON: I guess.

HELEN: I still wear that bracelet you bought me and Grainger is still certain he gave it to me. Every time he sees it he smiles happily.

> KATH *comes in from outside.* JENNY *goes to the kitchen to get some water.* KATH *sees* HELEN *sitting close to* DON *and frowns.* HELEN *pats him on the knee and gets up. She sits with* COOLEY. DON *remains sitting dejectedly. He realises the secret dream he has been nursing all these years is a fantasy.*

KATH: What were you two talking about?

DON: How children are a mixed blessing. You wouldn't be without 'em, but sometimes you wish you were.

> KATH *looks at him.*

What's wrong?

KATH: The two of you almost looked like man and wife.

DON: [*shaking his head*] We would've been sitting further apart.

KATH: [*sudden dawning on her*] You're still a bit keen on her, aren't you?

DON: Oh, come on. That was thirty-five years ago.

KATH: [*suspicious*] You looked…

DON: What?

KATH: Very cosy.

DON: [*mock earnestly*] It's about time you knew. I didn't run off with an ex student, I ran off with Helen, and I'm so glad I won't have to lie any longer.

> KATH *reads it as a joke as* DON *intended her to, shakes her head and walks off. Then looks across at* HELEN *and is suddenly struck by the thought that it probably was* HELEN. *She moves back to* DON.

What?

KATH: That student story never really convinced me. You couldn't even describe her accurately! She was blonde one time and a six months later she was dark.

DON: You don't seriously think—

KATH: It was Helen, wasn't it?

DON: [*horrified*] Of course not. I was joking.

KATH: The student was tall and willowy then a few years later she was five foot four.

DON: I was trying to disguise her true identity.

KATH: For God's sake, I'd *rather* it was Helen than some pubescent Lolita!

DON: Really?

KATH: Coming back to me after a week with Helen meant you actually sacrificed something for me. She was and is a substantial human being.

> DON *stares at her, nonplussed.*

DON: [*nodding forlornly*] Does this mean you're going to forgive and forget?

KATH: Of course not. I just won't bring it up as often.

> DON *seems grateful for even this slight improvement. She turns on her heel and leaves looking across at* HELEN *sitting next to* COOLEY. RICHARD *appears from the direction of the bedrooms.*

DON: How is she?

RICHARD: Fine. I'll just let her sleep a little then take her home.

> *There's a silence.*

[*Defensively*] Okay. She's a little over the top sometimes. It's better to feel strongly about things than feeling nothing.

> *They look at each other.*

I hoped that seeing how much I cared for her and she cared for me might have made a difference, but apparently not.

DON: Son, I need to say something to you whether you hate me for it or not.

RICHARD: What?

KATH: [*bursting out*] That woman is a nut case. Ask your father!

DON: I wasn't going to put it quite like that.

RICHARD: Dad, don't do your psychological thing with me.

KATH: Richard, she's got a hysterical personality disorder.

DON: Histrionic.

RICHARD: Everyone's infinitely complex. They can't be slotted into pigeonholes.

KATH: Your father knows what he's bloody well talking about.

RICHARD: She's volatile. I know that. It's nothing to do with personality disorders. She was brought up in a house where free expression of feelings were normal. Unlike Anglos who suppress everything.

DON: Listen to me. She's someone who has to be centre stage every moment of her life. If you can live with that, fine.

RICHARD: What a load of crap.

DON: She'll be manipulative, she'll demand attention and reassurance, and other people are going to find her a vain, self-centred pain in the arse.

RICHARD: Here we go again. Pigeonhole everyone and everything.

DON: And she could become an alcoholic or drug dependent.

RICHARD: What personality disorder is characterised by being pedantic, boring and judgemental? Because you've got it.

DON: [*with a shrug*] Okay.

RICHARD: Even if what you say is true, I do not care. I do not give a damn. That woman has made me feel truly alive for the first time in my life.

> *His mobile phone rings.* KATH *still has it so she hands it to him and he answers it.* BELLE *has heard it and comes in and listens.*

[*Into his phone*] Hello. You're awake. [*Beat.*] I can't understand anything when you're crying like that! [*Beat.*] Just calm down, will you. Calm down.

> *He tries to work out what she's saying. At that moment, hearing his voice,* ROBERTA *appears behind him in the doorway.*

Of course I still feel something for you. Good God, we've shared a life for nearly twenty years. I'm not a psychopath. I'm sorry about what happened, really sorry, because I know how much distress it's causing you all—but it did happen— [*Beat.*] Yes, what I've done might be a mistake. [*Beat.*] Of course I'll come and talk to you. But just not tonight.

BELLE: Dad! Don't be such an absolute bastard. Granny, will you take me? Now.

KATH: Of course.

BELLE: You get in your car and talk to her or I'll never speak to you again!

RICHARD: [*into his phone*] Alright. I'll come. I'll come, okay?

> *He ends the call and hands the phone back to* BELLE. ROBERTA, *whose eyes have been narrowing and whose body language has become more angry the more the conversation continued, launches herself at* RICHARD, *standing close to him and shouting.*

ROBERTA: It might be a mistake?! A mistake?! I've thrown away everything I had to be with you and it might be a mistake?!

RICHARD: Roberta…

ROBERTA: I was engaged to someone who was really crazy about me and I threw him over to be with you and now I find out it could all be a mistake. Now you're going straight off to your wife! The person you swore to me you no longer had any feelings for.

> BELLE *picks up a plate from the kitchen and hurls it at* ROBERTA. *It misses and smashes on the wall.*

BELLE: Get out of here, you witch! Go, right now!

RICHARD: Belle! You're behaving like a child.

ROBERTA: [*to* RICHARD] Did you mean the things you said or didn't you? Were all those things you told me lies!

RICHARD: No. Of course not.

> BELLE *picks up another plate but* DON *wrestles it off her.*

ROBERTA: Were they? [*She swivels around and faces* DON *and* KATH.] Are you pleased? All the poison you've poured into his ear about me has paid off. [*To* RICHARD] What's our so-called love been worth? Nothing. Precisely nothing. As far as you're concerned I've been just a convenient little dalliance before you run off home to your wife.

> *She picks up a plate and hurls it at* RICHARD. *It misses and she suddenly bursts into tears.*

KATH: Roberta, Tracy just tried to kill herself.

ROBERTA: I did too! And why? Because I love your son, and he knows it. And he knows that he loves me too. Richard, I can't take any more of this. You're going to have to choose.

RICHARD: Roberta, Tracy might try and kill herself again.

ROBERTA: And so might I. And if I do, you'll live with it for the rest of your life. If you're coming, come!

She storms towards the front door. He follows her.

RICHARD: Roberta!

She slams the door.

[*Shaken*] Jesus.

DON: Son, I know I'm a pedantic bastard, but she's not going to commit suicide.

RICHARD: How would you know?

DON: It's hard to hold centre stage if you're a corpse.

RICHARD: I love her. You don't understand, I love her.

BELLE *dives for another plate but* DON *is ready and disarms her.*

JENNY: [*quiet, but very firm*] Richard, the saddest thing about being a parent is that you know no matter what you say, your kids believe you know absolutely nothing that's relevant to their lives. Well, I'm not your parent, so listen to me.

MAL: Jenny, this isn't your business.

RICHARD: No more advice! I've had a gutful of advice.

JENNY: [*sternly*] Listen! Roberta is not an evil woman. At her core she's a desperate, needy little child. If you want to be her surrogate father, that's your choice.

RICHARD: Have all of you forgotten what passion is?

JENNY: That sort of passion. Frankly, yes. Long ago. But the passion I feel for my children floods through me day after day. If you lose the love of your children it's a huge price to pay.

There's a silence.

BELLE: Dad, you've got about twenty seconds left before you've lost mine.

RICHARD: Belle, that's terrible emotional blackmail.

BELLE: And what Roberta's doing isn't? Get in your car and talk to Mum!

RICHARD hesitates, torn. He looks at the door through which ROBERTA has departed then decides.

RICHARD: Will you come with me?

BELLE: No way! I'm going with Granny.

KATH: We'll see her in the morning, love. The people she needs now are you and Richard.

BELLE: [*to her father*] Alright, but we're going right now!

She starts towards the door and he follows. They go.

MAL: You've turned on some great election parties over the years, Don, but that gets my vote as the most entertaining since Cooley got whacked for porking the dentist's wife.

JENNY: Mal, what were the good qualities I once saw in you? Remind me please? [*To* KATH] I'd better go too.

KATH: It really was good you came. You're right. They never listen to parents, but he listened to you.

JENNY hugs KATH briefly.

JENNY: [*to* MAL] Don't forget Peter's birthday next week, and Lucy is launching her new business partnership next month. Oh, Kath, the food was delicious.

She goes.

MAL: I don't like to boast, but—

COOLEY: But you're just about to.

MAL: That kid of mine was being arrested in anti-globalisation rallies ten years ago and now she's grossing over four hundred thousand a year. Which I guess is peanuts compared to Richard, but then again Richard seems to have his problems.

HELEN: We must go too.

COOLEY has switched off the football and back to the election.

COOLEY: Hey, no. The next prime minister of this country is about to speak.

MAL: Abbott hasn't won yet!

COOLEY: He has, mate. Even if Gillard limps across the line her party has no policy. She'll be gone in a few months. The electorate know that Abbott will cut the debt, stop the boats, cut taxes and get this country moving again.

DON: Mate, this country is moving. Its unemployment rate is five per cent!

COOLEY: You're mob's stuffed, mate. The Greens are the new Opposition.

COOLEY *turns the sound up.*

KERRY O'BRIEN: [*TV, voice only*] We've sat here since six o'clock tonight to finally come to the conclusion at eleven-thirty that we haven't got a clue. If the great Australian public were bored witless by the campaign, by the end of it I think the only thing that was left of real interest was who was going to win. Here is Tony Abbot now.

We hear chants of 'Tony, Tony'.

It's a good thing he *is* fit because there's an awful lot of back slapping going on now. Here he is.

The 'Tony, Tony' chants grow in volume.

COOLEY: Those are real cheers, not the fake ones for Gillard.

TONY ABBOTT: [*TV, voice only*] Ladies and gentlemen, this is a night for pride in our achievements.

MAL: Pride? He couldn't even defeat Labor after the most politically disastrous three months in their history!

TONY ABBOTT: [*TV, voice only*] For satisfaction at the good results that have been achieved, but above all else, measured reflection on the magnitude of the task ahead.

MAL: The arrogant prick is speaking as if he's the next prime minister already!

COOLEY: He is. And he knows it.

TONY ABBOTT: [*TV, voice only*] There should be no premature triumphal-ism tonight—

MAL: Well, what the hell's that?

TONY ABBOTT: [*TV, voice only*] There should simply be an appreciation that this has been a great night for the Australian people.

MAL: Mate, get real! This has been one of the most shit nights in Australian political history!

COOLEY: The man your side said was unelectable has triumphed.

MAL: He hasn't been elected!

TONY ABBOTT: [*TV, voice only*] What is clear from tonight is that the Labor Party has definitely lost its majority.

> *Loud cheers.*

And what that means is that the government has lost its legitimacy!

> *More loud cheers.*

> MAL *switches the television off.*

COOLEY: Hey, leave it on!

MAL: There's no way I'm listening to any more of that shit!

COOLEY: They've lost, mate. Now or in a few months, they've lost.

> MAL *and* DON *look at each other. They both grudgingly think* COOLEY *is probably right. They turn savagely on the Labor Party.*

MAL: If they have, it's because they bloody well deserved to! I hate to agree with you but they haven't got an agenda.

DON: All they're about now is risk management. They stuffed up on pink batts, so total policy shutdown.

MAL: They caved in to the big polluters over the CPRS. They caved in to the miners over the Super Profits Tax.

DON: It's Tweedledum and Tweedledee. My economic reform's bigger than your economic reform.

MAL: False promises of endless prosperity. The crunch is coming, arseholes!

DON: Thank God I voted Green.

MAL: I've been doing it for twenty years.

COOLEY: Shut up and let me hear what our next prime minister is saying!

> COOLEY *starts wrestling* MAL *for the remote control. He gets short of breathe.* HELEN *knows the signs and races to put his mask over his face, administer oxygen, and sit him down.*

HELEN: Now will you please come, you idiot!

COOLEY: [*recovering*] Okay, okay. [*To* MAL] You want a lift?

MAL: And you have a blackout behind the wheel? I'll get a cab.

HELEN: Thanks Kath, Don.

> *She embraces them both.* MAL *lines up for his embrace which goes on a little too long.*

MAL: Helen, you are the best of the best. When the oxygen doesn't work anymore, give me a call.

COOLEY: The thought of that is going to keep me alive for the next ten years.

> COOLEY *takes his iPod off the stand, says goodbye to* DON *and* KATH *and leaves with* HELEN. DON *kisses her. He watches her wistfully and waves.* KATH *notices and is not impressed.*

KATH: Don, I'm going to bed. Mal, do you want me to call a cab?

MAL: I'd just like to sit here with Don for a few more moments and reflect on all the years that have passed.

> DON *raises his eyebrows despairingly behind* MAL'*s back and* KATH *laughs out loud. A shared moment between her and* DON. MAL *as ever is not picking up social signals.*

What's so funny?

KATH: [*almost affectionately*] You. Goodnight.

> MAL *gets up, his arms outstretched indicating he wants to give her a hug. Instead she blows him a kiss and disappears.* MAL *slumps down again and pours them both more red wine.*

MAL: Helen still feels something for me. I could tell.

DON: [*staring at him*] Mate, you are as thick as a brick.

> *They sit and stare at the television with its sound turned off, lit by the flicker of the screen.*

MAL: What's happened to this country in the last forty years? Fairness and decency has fought a battle with greed and greed has won. Abbott will do the bidding of big business, the mining giants and Rupert Murdoch, while the world marches headlong to Armageddon.

DON: The Greens control the Senate, mate.

MAL: Won't help.

DON: It's a sign, mate. It's a sign. All the verities are changing. There's no left and right anymore. The world is divided between those who believe something terrible is happening to our planet and those who are determined to party on.

MAL: Trouble is, mate, our generation were the ones that partied on.

DON: And I don't deny it, but the hope is with kids like Belle. They realise the party has to end and the way we live our lives has to change.

MAL: Shit.

DON: What?

MAL: Optimism. That's why I love you, mate. You look at those clouds of impending doom and you can still see a chink of light. Forty years on you can still see that chink of light. Except it wasn't just a chink back then. It was a full-on blinding flash of hope. Those were the days, Don. Those were the days.

DON gets up, puts his iPod in the stand and switches it on.

We hear Mary Hopkin singing 'Those Were the Days', starting at the chorus and continuing on as DON and MAL sit facing the flickering television.

THE END